The issues of policy examined in the final lecture are of political and practical importance in many underdeveloped countries. They include some of the major issues of public finance at the early stages of economic development, notably the framing of taxation to promote the expansion of the exchange economy, the implications of charging uniform freight rates and of flat-rate land taxes, the problems of transition from subsistence cultivation to production for wider exchange, certain of the problems of officially assisted industrialization as an instrument of economic development, the reform of the institutional structure in underdeveloped countries, and the principal political and economic issues of accelerated capital formation by means of compulsory saving.

P. T. BAUER is at present Smuts Reader in Commonwealth Studies, Cambridge University, and Fellow of Gonville and Caius College, Cambridge. He has held various teaching positions at London University and Cambridge University and has acted as visiting professor or visiting special lecturer at many universities in the United States. His publications on underdeveloped countries include a Cambridge economic handbook, *The Economics of the Under-developed Countries* (with B. S. Yamey), published in 1957; *West African Trade,* 1954; *The Rubber Industry,* 1948; and many articles in British, American, and Continental journals.

PUBLICATION NUMBER 4
Duke University Commonwealth-Studies Center

Economic Analysis and Policy
in Underdeveloped Countries

Duke University Commonwealth-Studies Center Publications

Economic Analysis and Policy
in Underdeveloped Countries

P. T. Bauer

Smuts Reader in Commonwealth Studies
Cambridge University
Fellow of Gonville and Caius College
Cambridge

PUBLISHED FOR THE

Duke University Commonwealth-Studies Center

DUKE UNIVERSITY PRESS, DURHAM, N. C.
CAMBRIDGE UNIVERSITY PRESS, LONDON

© 1957, Duke University Press

Cambridge University Press, London, N.W.1, England

Second printing, 1958

The Library of Congress has cataloged
this book as follows:

Bauer, Pèter Tamàs.
  Economic analysis and policy in underdeveloped countries.   Durham, N. C., Published for the Duke University
Commonwealth-Studies Center [by] Duke University Press,
1957.

  145 p.   21 cm.   (Duke University Commonwealth-Studies Center.
Publication no. 4)

  1. Underdeveloped areas.   2. Economic development.   I. Title.

HD82.B33   338.91   57–8814 ‡

Library of Congress   [5]

PRINTED IN THE UNITED STATES OF AMERICA

BY THE SEEMAN PRINTERY, INC., DURHAM, N. C.

FOREWORD

CONCERN WITH THE problems of underdeveloped
countries is most ancient. It manifests itself when-
ever some countries are considerably more advanced
than others and are recognized as being so, whether
on military or economic or yet other grounds. The
main centers of Hellenistic culture were so recognized and, later, Imperial Rome, her successor,
Byzantium, and Byzantium's flourishing city-state
neighbors. Subsequently, with the discovery of the
New World and the establishment of effective mari-
time communication with America and with south
and east Asia, northern and western Europe were
deemed to hold the relatively most advanced states,
together with the most progressive ways of producing and distributing goods. It was principally
from them that men and capital and advanced ways
of doing things flowed abroad, especially to the New
World. Because western Europe continued to progress absolutely and relatively, experiencing several
industrial revolutions and complementary socio-

political changes, it remained ascendant. From western Europe flowed most of the population, capital, and ideas that made possible the establishment of powerful economies in the New World; from western Europe too, flowed both the catalytic agents that gave rise to modern Japan, and capital and technology to facilitate the transformation of agrarian Europe. After World War I, and especially in the 1930's, the rate of flow of developmental agents from advanced countries (among which the United States had now come to be most outstanding) to less developed parts of the world diminished appreciably, only to experience a marked increase after World War II.

Recent political and social developments, especially since World War II, brought about a remarkable recrudescence of interest in economic development and a great strengthening of the belief, especially in underdeveloped countries, that the rate of economic growth must and could be greatly increased, especially through state intervention, and particularly if capital and technological assistance were to be had from abroad on easy terms. In this view advanced countries acquiesced in varying measure, in part because they believed the world would be politically more stable if the expanding aspirations of those living in less developed countries could be more fully realized.

During the past decade and a half a voluminous literature on underdeveloped countries, and on the theory of economic development, has come into being. Much information has been gathered over the period but the discussions still reflect wide differences of opinion. This diversity arises only in part from differences in the values stressed by authors and from differences in their points of view. Much of the divergence arises from the fact that very few authors are intimately acquainted with concrete situations in a number of distinct but somewhat comparable countries, and that many have very little close acquaintaince with empirical realities encountered in particular countries. It is only as the particular experiences of diverse underdeveloped economies become widely known and appreciated that the boundaries of consensus will be extended and the area of disagreement narrowed.

Undoubtedly the various writings of the author of this volume of lectures, now Smuts Reader in Commonwealth Studies at Cambridge University, will shed much light on the scene. He has devoted many years of study to specific economic aspects of underdeveloped countries in various parts of the world, especially in Africa and Asia. He is closely familiar, therefore, with many aspects of particular problems, with proposals for their solution, and with difficulties attendant upon efforts to carry out these proposals. He is completely at home in relevant contemporary economic theory and adept at utilizing this theory to analyze situations in underdeveloped countries, to formulate solutions, and to assess and choose among alternative proposals. His approach to the economic problems of underdeveloped countries is that of the scholar and the positive economist. His chief interest is in describing and analyzing phenomena; and, where appropriate, in showing how particular results emerge from specified changes in circumstances.

The language of these lectures is exact, terse, and deceptively simple. This may conceal the significance and originality of much of the argument in the discussion of method, in the analysis of underdeveloped economies, and in the examination of issues of policy. The discussion of the meaning of achievement of results in economic study and also of the relation between political position and the validity of economic propositions, the analysis of the ideas of the vicious circle of poverty and of the international demonstration effects, and the examination of the economic and political implications of compulsory saving—these are among the topics the treatment of which I believe to be both penetrating and original. And important as is the field of underdeveloped countries and economic development, the relevance of these topics extends far beyond it and their illuminating treatment opens up wide areas of discussion. These topics and much more will be found by the reader in the concise, well-written, and precise lectures that follow. Should his appetite be whetted for yet more, whether along the lines of these lectures, or along somewhat different lines, he may turn to the works included in the select bibliography that appears just after the closing lecture.

Since the Commonwealth-Studies Center is concerned exclusively with the encouragement of research, specific theories or interpretations of Commonwealth affairs appearing in these publications do not constitute an expression of the view of the Center or of the Carnegie Corporation, which has furnished financial support to the Center. The respective authors of the several publications are responsible for the conclusions expressed in them.

JOSEPH J. SPENGLER

INTRODUCTORY STATEMENT

I SHOULD LIKE to thank Duke University for the honor of the invitation extended to me as visiting lecturer to the Commonwealth-Studies Center.

The honor of this invitation, and the quality of the first set of lectures delivered in 1955 by Professor Underhill,[1] imposed a special obligation, both in the choice of suitable subjects, and in the manner in which they were to be discussed. The British Commonwealth is not an economic unit in any meaningful sense; and, further, the differences between its members in economic structure and in stages of economic development are too far-reaching for a general economic treatment of the Commonwealth to be illuminating. I was tempted to discuss the economic development of part of the Commonwealth, or to examine one or other of its major economic institutions. I felt, however, that by a rather different approach I could serve better the purpose of the

1. Frank H. Underhill, *The British Commonwealth: An Experiment in Co-operation among Nations* (Durham, N. C., 1956).

Commonwealth-Studies Center, and also treat of subjects of wider interest.

Over five-sixths of the population of the Commonwealth, and three-quarters of the population of the world, live in underdeveloped countries, to accept the term which in spite of much valid criticism is still convenient to describe countries in which real income and capital per head are low compared to those in North America, western Europe and Australasia; in which a large part of output is destined for the direct satisfaction of the wants of the producer and of his family rather than for wider exchange or sale; and in which there is as yet no large-scale application of the fruits of technological advance to the arts of agriculture and industry.[2] The countries of the Commonwealth represent a substantial and heterogeneous part of the underdeveloped world.

Over the last two decades there has been a great upsurge (or rather resurgence) of discussion

2. The underdeveloped countries thus defined comprise about three-quarters of the population of the world, and they form a very heterogeneous collection. References herein to development are to the development of these countries rather than to the growth of more advanced economies.

The diversity in the underdeveloped world and the implications of this diversity for the possibilities of generalization are considered in some detail in a recently published Cambridge Economic Handbook, *The Economics of Under-developed Countries* (London, 1957), by B. S. Yamey and myself. Several of the topics in these lectures are developed more fully in that book.   Over the last five years I have worked very closely with Mr. Yamey. The general argument of these lectures owes much to this collaboration and thus to Mr. Yamey. Apart from the benefits I have derived from this close collaboration, I am also indebted to him for many specific suggestions and improvements in the course of the preparation of these lectures.

of the economics of development and of under-developed countries. This provides the theme of my lectures. The first deals with the scope, method, and possibilities of economics in the study of under-developed countries, as well as with the repercussions on economics of the increased interest in under-developed countries. The second deals with some characteristic features of the economic landscape in underdeveloped countries. The third examines certain issues of policy. I shall discuss features of the economic landscape and aspects of economic develop-ment in a number of Commonwealth countries, but they will serve as illustrations rather than as prin-cipal themes.

CONTENTS

CONTENTS

*Economic Analysis and Policy
in Underdeveloped Countries*

Our trouble is not ignorance it is just that we
know so many things that are not true.

JOSH BILLINGS

We need to cultivate the restraint of Galileo,
who left the world of angels and spirits until
the time should come when it could be explored, and contented himself with such principles as he could extract with confidence from
experience, though the resolution committed
him to such trivialities as the timing of balls
rolling down grooves. It is that self-control
—the voluntary restriction to the task of extending knowledge outwards from the observed to the unobserved instead of imposing
imagined universal principles inwards on the
world of observation—that is the essential
hallmark of the man of science, distinguishing
him most fundamentally from the non-scientific philosopher. H. DINGLE

The Economic Study of Underdeveloped Countries

> More than other scientists, social scientists need to be self-conscious about their methodology.
> MILTON FRIEDMAN

> The discovery of intimate true affinities between things which appear wholly different to the hasty observer, has long been recognized as one of the chief tasks of physical science.
> ALFRED MARSHALL

IN THE LAST TWO DECADES there has been a great upsurge of interest in the economics of underdeveloped countries. Although it is related to the political developments of the period, I believe that the increased interest is not merely ephemeral but is likely to be lasting. This is suggested, for instance, by the fact that it represents essentially a resumption of the interest of the classical economists rather than a complete break with tradition. The obvious political and practical importance of the issues involved, the large sums available for this branch of study, the intellectual interest of many of the phenomena and problems, all suggest that the interest is likely to persist.

The economic study of underdeveloped countries is certain to bear on important issues of policy, and it may possibly make valuable practical contributions. It may also advance economics by extending the range of phenomena over which its hypotheses can be examined and new hypotheses developed. But quite possibly the contribution of economics to policy may be negligible, or even negative, if its pronouncements obscure rather than illuminate issues. Work in this field may also undermine economics as a systematic discipline. Interest in the practical problems of what were in effect underdeveloped countries stimulated the emergence of economics as a systematic discipline. It may well be that the same interest will contribute to its disintegration, or at least to its transformation into a subject radically different from economics as it was known until recently. The grounds for these expressions of hope and fear will, I trust, become clearer at a later stage.

Economists are generally reluctant to discuss questions of scope and method. Protracted concern with questions of method is indeed apt to be fruitless and tiresome, somewhat akin to the excessive introspection characteristic of certain types of neurosis. But the healthy extrovert who never questions or examines himself can also be a bore, uncritical and unaware of his potentialities and limitations, and insensitive to his impact on others. Occasional self-examination and spells of introspection are invaluable both to individuals and to intellectual disciplines, particularly when they are about to branch out into unaccustomed spheres of activity.

For some time the prevailing opinion among economists has been that we should get on with our work, and that the results of the work will serve as a test of the value and usefulness of the methods employed. Unfortunately, however, reference to achievement of results does not offer a worthwhile test or criterion of method in economics, because this expression has acquired several quite different meanings: correct establishment of functional relationships; successful forecasting of future events; ability to influence policy, whether generally or in the attainment of a particular aim; and other meanings as well. Obviously these do not provide a simple criterion of method.

Economists often act as advisers to governments or to businessmen, and the tasks imposed by this function have served to aggravate the confusion of the different interpretations of the achievement of results in our subject. Such ambiguities do not arise in the natural or logical sciences. The achievement of natural scientists is not usually judged by the value, wisdom, or efficacy of their advice to governments, but by their contribution to the establishment of propositions of depth and generality about natural phenomena. It is only in the social sciences that ambiguity arises in the aims of the discipline as between the establishment of generalizations and the results of courses of action which may have been influenced by these generalizations. And this affects economics particularly, because economists, much more than other social scientists, act as advisers on policy.

The ambiguities are removed, or at least greatly disminished, if we remember the distinctions between positive economics, normative economics, and the art of political economy, clearly drawn by J. N. Keynes in his now little-read but excellent book, *The Scope and Method of Political Economy*,[1] and recently re-emphasized by Professor Milton Friedman in his paper "The Methodology of Positive Economics."[2] Keynes distinguishes between "a positive science . . . [,] a body of systematized knowledge concerning what is; a normative or regulative science . . . [,] a body of systematized knowledge discussing criteria of what ought to be . . . ; an art . . . [,] a system of rules for attainment of a given end."[3] To put it briefly, propositions of positive economics refer to what is, those of normative economics to what ought to be, and those of the art of political economy to the means for obtaining specified results.

The propositions of positive economics, normative economics, and the art of economics, or the art of political economy as it is sometimes termed, are logically distinct. Positive economics, however, has primacy, in the sense that the most significant and

1. London, 1891.
2. In *Essays in Positive Economics* (Chicago, 1953). Although I disagree with some of the argument, I believe this paper is fundamental.
3. *Op. cit.*, pp. 34-35.

distinctive contributions the economist can make to normative economics and to the art of economics or of political economy stem from the generalizations established by positive economics. To take perhaps the simplest example, if it is desired to curtail the consumption of a particular commodity the economist may suggest that it should be taxed; this would be based on the generalization that the quantity demanded varies inversely with price.

In the remainder of this lecture, and throughout the next, I shall deal almost entirely with positive economics. In my last lecture I shall deal with both positive and normative propositions, as well as with matters which belong to the art of political economy, and I shall try to keep these distinct; unless the contrary is stated, reference to economic generalization in these lectures is to positive economics.

Economics seeks to establish generalizations by observing and analyzing apparently diverse phenomena to detect uniformities underlying their diversity. The establishment of generalizations makes possible, where appropriate, the prediction of the probable consequences of specified occurrences, conditions, or circumstances.

As is well known, the task of the economist is complicated by the multiplicity of forces acting simultaneously on the phenomena he investigates, and by the impossibility of eliminating some of these by means of a controlled or, more exactly, a contrived experiment. If there were not so many and often complex and varying forces operating simultaneously, the impossibility of contrived experiments would not be important—witness the precision attained by astronomy, geology, and some other observational but non-experimental sciences.

The economist has to rely very largely on uncontrolled experience.[4] This is available in great volume, and quite often in a form exhibiting functional relationships almost as clearly as does a contrived experiment. Here is but one of many examples. In recent years in Nigeria some of the official marketing boards have offered special premiums for particular grades of the products which they have the sole right to export; and this has resulted in a spectacular increase in the production of these particular grades. This episode reflects a recognition of the functional relationship between supply and price, and it also confirms this relationship. The need to rely on uncontrolled experiences does, however, increase the number of observations required, and also complicates their successful analysis and interpretation, before we can discern successfully the significant uniformities and ascertain their limits. However, in spite of these difficulties many highly successful generalizations have been established. These include the inverse relationship between price and quantity demanded (the law of demand); the positive response of the supply of an individual commodity to a change in

4. Introspection is a supplementary source of information which at times can be suggestive.

price; Gresham's Law; the dependence of the division of labor on the extent of the market; the tendency of individuals to turn to activities yielding the highest net advantage within the opportunities open to them.

The absence of contrived experiment affects the firmness of the various generalizations in different degrees. For example, it does not affect at all the proposition that if the price rises sufficiently the quantity demanded must diminish, and after a point more than proportionately to the increase in price; and similarly for the converse response of the supply of an individual commodity to a fall in price. These propositions follow from the universally observed limitation of incomes and from the presence of costs (i.e., ultimately from the limitation of resources), and they are quite general. In other instances the confidence with which generalizations can be proposed, and the width of their applicability, are affected by the absence of contrived experiment.

But the absence of this device has a further, and in practice very important, result to which Professor Friedman has drawn attention. He points out that the absence of the vivid and dramatic evidence provided by the contrived experiment adds greatly to the difficulty of securing acceptance for generalizations which are amply justified by analysis of the available evidence. He writes: "It renders the weeding-out of unsuccessful hypotheses slow and difficult. They are seldom downed for good and are always cropping up again."[5]

5. *Op. cit.*, p. 11.

This is only too true. The functional relationships
between price and quantity demanded, and between
price and the supply of particular products, are among
the most elementary generalizations of our subject,
which moreover often serve as bases for policy. Yet in
recent years it has been argued by some professional
economists that the imposition of export duties at
high rates has not affected the supply of the products
on which they were levied; and that the effects on
the quantities demanded of the imposition or increase
even of heavy import duties over the entire range of
imports, including luxuries, can be ignored.[6]

Two important and related distinctions must be
remembered in the framing and testing of economic
generalizations. The first is the distinction between
a functional relationship and a historical sequence of
events. The law of demand is not invalid because in
a boom both the prices and the quantities sold of many
commodities are higher than in a depression. Again,
the fact that the exports of some of the commodities
subject to heavy export taxes in Africa have not de-
clined compared to an earlier period does not affect
the conclusion that this taxation has affected supply,
especially long-period supply. Second, prediction, in
the sense of the assessment of the results of specified
occurrences or conditions, must be distinguished from
the forecasting of future events. Even if the pre-

6. Examples will be found in the references in an article by
Professor F. W. Paish and myself, "The Reduction of Fluctua-
tions in the Incomes of Primary Producers Further Considered,"
Economic Journal, LXIV (Dec. 1954), especially pp. 707-709,
and in an exchange between Mr. John H. Adler and myself in the
Journal of Political Economy, LXIV (Oct. 1956), 425-441.

diction that the producers of a particular crop respond to a higher price by producing more is correct, this prediction does not enable us to forecast accurately next year's output (still less the harvest in the more distant future), which in the event will be affected by many factors besides changes in price. You will appreciate that in this sense prediction and explanation are, as Marshall has reminded us, the same operation (the establishment of uniformities) in opposite directions. The confusion between these two different meanings of prediction (that is between assessment of the probable results of specified occurrences and forecasting of unknown future events) which is rife in the contemporary literature, notably on underdeveloped countries, does not usually arise in academic discussion outside the social sciences. Such simple confusions underline the value of occasional reflection on method.

The depth and significance of economic generalizations depend on the quality of the underlying observation and analysis. In certain branches of economics, notably in the study of underdeveloped countries, the importance of direct observation and the importance of the quality of observation have been underrated in recent years. By direct observation I mean, in this context, gathering of information personally or reliance on comparatively unprocessed material, such as files of business firms and government departments, locally published reports (which are generally nearer to unprocessed material than reports published in metropolitan countries on the basis of local reports), proceedings of representative assemblies, newspapers, advertisements, market reports, auction notices, and the like. Some of the reasons for the decline of direct observation lie outside economics, and I shall leave these on one side. In economics itself various influences have contributed to it. Preoccupation with formal theory has been one such factor. Another factor has been the emphasis on quantification, in the sense of study of those aspects of the economy which can be expressed readily in the form of statistics, in fact or at least in appearance. This second factor is sufficiently important to warrant some discussion.

Statistics are obviously indispensable in many branches of economic study; there are many fields of the subject in which the most important and relevant factors and aspects can be helpfully quantified. In many other fields, however, reliance on statistics alone, at least in their conventional form unsupported by other forms of evidence, especially more direct observation, is insufficient. For example, the dependence of producers on a particular crop cannot meaningfully be measured by the proportion of income, or of cash income, derived from it, since it is also affected by the ease with which they can turn to alternative activities, and this cannot be inferred from statistics. The meaning of the flow of goods and services known as the national income is much affected by such considerations and factors as the proportion of output purchased by the government out of the proceeds of taxation, as distinct from purchases by individuals out of freely disposable income; the presence of extensive rationing in contrast to the ready availability of goods and services at market prices; the presence of direction over the factors of production, in contrast to the absence of such specific direction. Again, a specified measure of inequality of income has a different significance when the composition of the various income groups is stable, and when their composition is changing rapidly.

Thus not only is the quantification of a situation necessarily an abstraction, but it may also be unrepresentative of some of its most important aspects. While the emphasis on statistics has resulted in much greater exactness in some parts of economics, in others it has acted as a poor substitute, rather than as a support, for careful observation and clear thinking. This again is particularly evident in discussion on underdeveloped countries. The expense and difficulty of visiting these countries, and especially of carrying out sustained local investigations, has undoubtedly contributed to the reliance on statistics, and to the emphasis on those aspects of their economic life which can be quantified meaningfully or conveniently or plausibly, and which in that form are then accessible to all without firsthand observation or detailed enquiry. The neglect of such observation and enquiry has in turn concealed the limitations of this type of information. I remember my astonishment at seeing the large volume of trading activity in West Africa when trade, according to the occupational statistics, was an insignificant occupation. This observation led me to doubt the empirical and analytical bases of some widely accepted propositions about the relation between economic progress and occupational distribution.

Direct observation is likely to be especially valuable in economics because of the practical absence of contrived experiments, and also because of the limitations of statistical evidence, which stem both from the absence of reliable statistics and, more fundamentally, from the difficulty or even impossibility of meaningful quantification of significant aspects of a situation. These considerations apply in differing degrees to the different fields of economic study. Observation needs to play only a comparatively small part in demography, in most of aggregative analysis, and in the establishment of some of the simplest propositions of supply and demand analysis which are a corollary of the limitation of resources. However, when we wish to go beyond these, direct observation is often necessary for the discernment of uniformities, particularly in suggesting hypotheses, and in drawing attention both to significant features of economic life and to the limitations of other forms of evidence. And this applies in very special measure to the economics of underdeveloped countries, in view both of the unfamiliarity of the landscape and of the severe limitations of statistical evidence.

How far do the generalizations of economics, evolved in the West on the basis of societies permeated by a money economy and largely individualistic and industrialized, apply in underdeveloped countries? The crude objection that the very existence of differences invalidates these generalizations can be dismissed easily; the discernment of uniformities underlying diversities is the primary task of scientific enquiry. But, of course, the differences may be too deep-seated for the establishment of valid generalizations. Let me first state my own position on this baldly. I am now convinced of the very wide applicability to underdeveloped countries of the basic methods of approach of economics and of the more elementary conclusions stemming from these. I am thinking especially of the elements of supply and demand analysis and its simpler conclusions, the tendency of people to seek activities and occupations which yield the highest net advantage within the opportunities open to them, the implications of the concept of complementary and competitive relationships between productive resources, and many others. Some of these propositions are direct corollaries of the limitation of resources, so that their wide applicability to underdeveloped countries is not in question.

Those who dispute the relevance of the propositions of economics to underdeveloped countries usually base their arguments on the differences in attitudes and institutions between the underdeveloped world and the western countries. Usually, however, these views reflect incomplete observation or imperfect understanding of economics. A few years ago in the Gold Coast a highly placed civil servant told me that his experience had convinced him that economics was irrelevant in Africa, because the African simply did not respond to economic motives. I asked him what all the cocoa trees were doing in the Gold Coast, since about two million acres are under cocoa in that country, every tree owned, planted, and worked by Africans. He was slightly taken aback, and proceeded to argue that it was clear from market conditions in the Gold Coast that as a consumer at any rate the African was utterly irrational, because he insisted on a particular brand of bicycle (a Raleigh bicycle) and refused all others, though these were really not inferior. In fact, the prevailing situation illustrated the high response of the Africans to price changes and price differences. The Raleigh bicycle was the only brand of bicycle subject to price control in the Gold Coast. The price control was partly effective in the stores of the European and Levantine merchants. In the open markets where African resellers operated it was ineffective, and there these bicycles were freely obtainable at the higher equilibrium price. As everybody who obtained a price-controlled bicycle could promptly resell it at the higher price, the merchants were besieged with demands for this brand, not only from people who wanted them for their own use, but also from actual and prospective resellers, a situation familiar from experience elsewhere. There were no difficulties in the buying and selling of other brands which were not price controlled; and, as was clear from import statistics, the Africans used very large numbers of these other bicycles.

Let me give you another example of the argument of the alleged irrelevance of economics to under-developed countries, an example which also provides a curious instance of self-refutation by the exponent of the argument. A year or so ago I attended a small conference at which a distinguished and highly placed Indian addressed a group on some problems of Indian economic policy. He reminded us that the values and responses of the great majority of Indians differed fundamentally from those of people in the West, notably in that Indians had a strong leaning towards asceticism, as was shown by the deep respect felt for Gandhi. He then went on to say that government control both of imports and of the use of capital was essential, because without it higher incomes would attract luxury or semi-luxury imports, and scarce capital resources would be absorbed by uses yielding the highest profit, which were likely to be the construction of cinemas, the manufacture of soft drinks, and the like. Somewhat surprisingly, the obvious inconsistency was perceived neither by the distinguished speaker nor by the majority of the audience.

Of course the institutional framework of the community limits and directs the operations of its economic activities; and this framework in under-developed countries is often very different from that in developed countries. This is seen in such matters as the values which people cherish and thus in the objectives they wish to attain, and in the various social and technical obstacles which circumscribe their activities. Whether it is more or less restrictive than in the West is doubtful, nor is it certain that this is a meaningful question.[7] The meaningful and relevant question is whether the hypotheses of economics yield successful explanations and predictions under these different conditions. I am convinced that they do, even though it is often difficult to recognize the familiar responses when these take place in a strange institutional setting, especially when the values of the people and their pattern of consumption (especially the type of expenditure likely to secure social distinction) differ greatly from ours, and when the institutional barriers to movement also differ from those to which we are accustomed. But all this does not invalidate the propositions of economics. There are several million followers of the Mosaic law in the United States and elsewhere in the West who do not eat pig-meat. We do not say that the law of demand is invalid because they do not eat more pork when its price falls. Nor do the various institutional obstacles to movement invalidate the propositions of economics. There are institutional barriers to movement in developed countries also. Indeed, quite often such obstacles are themselves evidence of the operation of the familiar responses: they are fre-

7. The lower level of capital and income does restrict the range of effective alternatives in underdeveloped countries much more than in developed countries, but this limitation is quite different from the institutional restrictions considered in the text.

quently required to maintain a level of prices or incomes which would be jeopardized by additional supplies which would be attracted in the absence of these obstacles.

Here are two examples to illustrate both the operation of these responses and the need to adjust our eyes to an unfamiliar landscape.

India is often instanced as a country where the rigid dictates of religion, custom, and caste invalidate the propositions of economics. South India, especially rural Madras, is, or at least was until a few years ago, the stronghold of caste. Before the Second World War the occupations which people in the villages could pursue were largely determined by their caste. There were in consequence wide differences in earnings and net advantages between occupations which were largely unrelated to skill. But within the opportunities open to them the custom-dominated and caste-bound people responded rapidly and markedly to differences in incomes and net advantages. This was shown, for instance, by their great readiness to migrate, especially to the rubber and tea estates in Malaya and Ceylon, and by their prompt reaction to changes in economic conditions in these countries, changes of which the illiterate villagers of rural Madras, scores or even hundreds of miles from the ports, and about fifteen hundred miles from Malaya, were remarkably well-informed. For example, during the severe depression of the early 1930's migration to Malaya ceased because of the heavy fall in the volume of employment on estates. When conditions improved in 1933-34, the recruiting depots maintained by the Malayan authorities in two ports in Madras were besieged by tens of thousands of would-be migrants who had heard in up-country Madras that employment was available again in Malaya. Altogether this migration provides much information on economic response. An example may be illuminating. On the terms offered by the employers there was an excess of would-be migrants over the number of vacancies on estates; for the numbers required the remuneration offered exceeded the supply price, so that there was an element of rent in the wage rate. The vacancies had to be rationed. Preference in employment and in the provision of migrants' passages was given to applicants holding some sort of letter of invitation from the estates or from relatives already employed there. These letters became, in effect, negotiable instruments, and were bought, sold, and forged—and this among the custom-bound illiterate population of some of the poorest and most backward areas in India.[8]

My other example is from East Africa, where, in the interior of Kenya, British administration was established about the turn of the century. Much of this area was very backward, even by African standards. As is usual, the establishment of settled gov-

8. The general practice of the various Indian administrations in protecting or otherwise subsidizing economic activities they wish to encourage also implies a recognition of the familiar economic responses. For instance, assistance was extended in the 1930's to cane sugar production in India and this brought about a rapid increase in the acreage under this crop. This is only one of many examples.

ernment was accompanied by the introduction of taxation, such as hut taxes and the like. Because of the undeveloped state of the economy some of the backward tribes were at first allowed to pay the taxes in cattle, which were then resold in towns by government agents. This method had to be abandoned, because the Africans paid in old beasts and the animals died on the collectors' hands. This illustrates a response designed to minimize cost. But it also provides a remarkable confirmation of Gresham's Law. Bad money drives out good, even if money takes the form, or reverts to the form, of cattle.

For obvious reasons of time and space I cannot multiply examples. There is available a great volume of evidence, general as well as specific and detailed evidence, of the pronounced response of producers, consumers, and intermediaries to prices, price differences and price changes in the underdeveloped countries of the Commonwealth. Much of this relates to areas where on general grounds one might expect these responses to be weak or largely absent: to India, the stronghold of caste and custom, and to Africa and Malaya, where the indigenous populations have been drawn only comparatively recently into a wider system of exchange. And much of it illustrates prompt and sensitive responses to small differences in prices, or arbitrage transactions, or responses in anticipation of expected changes in prices.[9]

9. Mr. Charles Wilson writes in *The History of Unilever* (London, 1954), "The mills [Lever's African oil mills] . . . were wholly dependent on local supplies of nuts. The natives knew when supplies at the mills were running low, held back supplies

The alleged inflexibility of wants of the local population, especially in Africa and Malaysia, is another ground on which the irrelevance of economics to underdeveloped countries is sometimes urged. Of course, even a static pattern of wants would not destroy the relevance of economics, because the population would presumably wish to satisfy these wants with least effort, and this at once restores the relevance of our subject. In fact, however, the allegation of static wants is palpably unfounded. It can be easily disproved for these populations on the basis of such readily accessible and obvious information as the rapid increase with economic advance in the volume, range, and variety of imports in Africa and Malaya and elsewhere, and the similar increase in the consumption of commodities subject to excise duties for which the statistics are readily available. The spread of the cultivation of cash crops and, to a lesser extent, the acceptance of wage-earning employment in these countries, are both evidence of the flexibility of wants and also instruments in the economic advance which has taken place: these are the activities which have provided the incomes for the purchase of imported

---

and put up their prices accordingly" (p. 182).

The withholding of supplies by African producers and intermediaries in anticipation of higher prices has in recent years been a feature of the operations of the West African marketing boards often noted in their annual reports. These reports also frequently refer to the prompt response of Africans to price differences, notably to the readiness to adjust the production of different grades to the price differentials offered. A number of examples are quoted in my article in the *Journal of Political Economy*, October 1956, already mentioned.

merchandise. The easily observable response in the volume of imports to changes in the flow of money income in these territories in turn shows that not only are wants not static, but that expenditure both on consumption goods and on simple equipment often responds fairly promptly to changes in income.

The readiness of response varies with all sorts of factors and influences, and for various reasons there may well be lulls in the growth of the demand for goods and services. In stable and stratified societies with strong traditions wants may be less expansive than in other more fluid societies. People in contact with foreigners with a higher standard of living may adjust their standard of living more readily than do people in more self-contained societies. Further, the supply of effort may at times, and over certain ranges of income, diminish with a higher income (the backward-rising supply curve of effort). But this is familiar in the West, and is not held to invalidate the generalizations of economics.[10]

The influence of custom on the adjustment of wants and on the readiness to shift between activities varies in different underdeveloped countries. It also varies between ethnic groups, and even in the same ethnic

10. In underdeveloped countries, much as elsewhere, the nature of the response of the supply of effort to a change in remuneration depends generally on the relative impact of the change on marginal income and on total income, and also on various factors influencing the substitution between work in the exchange sector and in the subsistence sector and between work and leisure. These influences are discussed in an article by Professor F. W. Paish, "Economic Incentive in Wartime," *Economica*, August 1941, and P. T. Bauer and B. S. Yamey, *op. cit.*, chap. vii.

group at different times. All of this, of course, applies generally in the West also. The force of custom is generally not so strong nor so pervasive to limit these responses sufficiently to deprive economics of its relevance. The payment of bride prices in Africa is deeply rooted in tribal custom. If there are any prices which could be expected to be fixed by custom and to be totally unresponsive to changed relations of supply and demand, it would be bride prices. In fact, however, these vary appreciably with economic conditions. In Nigeria, for example, there was a general rise in bride prices after the Second World War. And there, as elsewhere in Africa, attempts were made by the native authorities to control them, which proved ineffective in the absence of a suitable system of rationing.

In underdeveloped countries, as in developed countries, adjustments are often effected through changes in quantity and quality, while the nominal price remains unchanged. Marshall noticed this for India:

For instance, in 1878, when the taxes on salt were readjusted throughout India, being raised in the southern half and lowered in the northern, it was expected by many that the rule of custom and the smallness of retail purchases would prevent the raiyat from feeling the change for a long time to come. But the result was opposite. Salt was retailed by the pinch. And from the day when the new rule came into operation, the pinch was increased in size in the northern, and diminished in the southern half.[11]

11. *Memorials of Alfred Marshall*, ed. Pigou (London, 1925), p. 356.

This type of observation may have induced Marshall to say, in his inaugural lecture at Cambridge:

In fact after examining in detail the prices of the chief purchases made by the peasants in some parts of India, I have come to the conclusion that fixed custom has less to do with them than is the case with the agricultural labourer in the south of England.[12]

I found many examples in West Africa of substantial differences between actual and nominal prices. Quite often, of course, apparently rigid prices do indeed reflect maintained prices; and detailed enquiry is often necessary to ascertain the content of price quotations.

I hope that these examples will make clearer the reasons for my earlier insistence on the importance of direct observation as a source of information. The discernment of uniformities and the recognition of the operation of familiar tendencies in an unfamiliar setting require extensive reliance on direct observation and the exercise of imagination, as well as a firm grounding in elementary economics. The exercise of imagination, as distinct from fantasy, is generally stimulated by observation and experience, as these often suggest new lines of enquiry as well as previously unnoticed or unsuspected relevant connections between phenomena. Reliance on direct observation makes one independent of the activities of the processor of the data. In this field the activities of the processor are often difficult to assess from afar—afar

12. *Ibid.* p. 170.

not only in term of physical distance, but also in terms of differences in institutions of the underdeveloped countries and those of the West, and differences in the aims and methods of the processor and the investigator. The value of unprocessed material is not necessarily a function of its truth in the accepted sense of the term. For instance, advertisements are not usually considered as media for the disinterested dissemination of truth. But a reading of advertisements in the African press immediately dispels any notion that African wants are static.

The particular merit of personal observation or the use of unprocessed material is relevant to many different aspects of the study of underdeveloped economies. For example, this type of information suggests that a large proportion of the output in many underdeveloped countries is produced for consumption by the producer and his family or by other narrowly limited groups (loosely termed subsistence production), and that the extension of the exchange economy is a necessary condition of economic development. This in turn leads to the recognition of the relevance of the prospect of a higher and more varied level of consumption as an inducement to production for the market. This conclusion then bears on the hypothesis, advanced by Professor Ragnar Nurkse, that contact with more advanced countries is likely to retard economic development by encouraging new wants and discouraging saving and investment, an important but somewhat paradoxical suggestion which I shall examine in my second lecture. Again, direct

observation leads one to question the widely accepted
hypothesis that the proportion of the occupied population in the service industries is a simple positive
function of the level of economic development, of
which it is said to offer a convenient index. The empirical basis of this argument is furnished by occupational statistics. These are, however, of very limited
value in the usual conditions of imperfect specialization in underdeveloped counties.

For these reasons it is not surprising that competent
studies based on personal experience or on the use
of unprocessed material[13] generally contrast strikingly
with the great bulk of current literature on underdeveloped countries, which even when not blatantly
merely political is obviously based on statistical or
other summary statements the value and limitations
of which the writers cannot assess.

Much of the current discussion on underdeveloped
countries is vitiated by treating supply and demand
as physical quantities unaffected by price, and, perhaps more generally, by regarding quantities as fixed
or given, and not as variables. This widespread

13. An excellent example of a study embodying the results of
such work is an article, "Jute Production Policies in India and
Pakistan," *Indian Economic Journal*, July 1955, by Dr. F. C.
Shorter of the University of California. This paper illuminates
important features of the economic landscape of India and
Pakistan, which are, moreover, of general interest; it has much
to contribute to policy; and it contains a valuable discussion on
both formal and substantive levels of the assessment of the
elasticity of demand for a particular export crop of an individual country.

Some other examples of such studies are mentioned in the
reading list at the end of this book.

practice strikes at the root of economics as a distinct discipline and threatens to transform it into a branch of production engineering. I shall illustrate in the subsequent lectures the relevance in particular contexts of the neglect of these simple functional relationships. Similarly, I shall consider later some implications of discussing underdeveloped countries in a timeless and unhistorical manner, without reference even to recent economic history, a widespread and misleading practice which is plainly inappropriate in discussions of underdeveloped countries and of economic development. I shall now deal at somewhat greater length with certain other aspects and problems of method, relevant both to the study of underdeveloped countries and also to that of many other branches of economics.

Attempts to forecast unknown future events have become a familiar feature of economic discussion, and are now prominent in discussions on underdeveloped countries. As I have already said, forecasting of the unknown future must be distinguished from prediction in the sense of assessment of the probable results of specified occurrences or conditions, an activity or exercise which is a corollary of successful generalization.

Forecasting of some kind is indispensable in politics, administration and business, and is therefore likely to be important among the tasks of economists in the service of government and business. In scientific enquiry forecasting is generally a derivative of prediction in the technical sense of the term, in that

the correct assessment of the probable results of specified occurrences may promote more reliable forecasts than would be possible otherwise. But forecasting is not an appropriate major function of economics, or of any other serious discipline. It does not
usually attempt to establish uniformities of behavior,
or even to represent a step towards their establishment. It does not advance knowledge or promote
understanding in any serious sense, and thus does not
contribute to economics or to any other systematic
body of knowledge. In fact, so far from promoting
knowledge it is more likely to obscure issues and
divert attention from serious study. It often serves
as a cloak for a failure to undertake the sustained,
serious effort of observation and analysis which is required for the discernment of uniformities of behavior and clear statement of functional relationships.
For instance, it is not accidental that the authors of
the report of the International Bank on Nigeria[14]
should try to guess the future course of prices many
years forward, but fail to mention anywhere in their
lengthy report the effects of prices or price changes
on either supply or demand, not even in the context
of proposals for the imposition of import and export duties at high rates. In general, in economic
discussions in which forecasts are prominent demand
and supply are frequently treated as simple physical
quantities and not as variables which are functions
of price. The demand for these forecasts often stems
from deep-seated psychological motives, and it is

14. *The Economic Development of Nigeria* (Baltimore, 1955).

frequently unrelated to the accuracy of the forecasts. A great upsurge of interest in forecasting is usually evidence of an unhealthy state of mind, especially of a readiness to welcome panaceas. I believe also that the great increase in the demand for these forecasts, even by educated people, and the great prestige of their purveyors are symptoms and harbingers of very deep-seated social and political transformations. A sudden resurgence in the activities and prestige of oracles and soothsayers in the Roman Empire in the second and third centuries testified to the decline in critical outlook and to the emergence of credulity, which prepared the way both for the acceptance of a new faith from the East and for the collapse of order, civilization, and even material well-being.[15]

The modest intellectual status and content of this activity are often overrated. In the literature on underdeveloped countries forecasting is widely regarded as a notable or even indispensable factor in the framing of rational economic policy, as well as a major instrument for the advancement of knowledge about these countries.

15. "The oracles that had been silenced were heard again; the astrologers swarmed in every city; the philosophers were surrounded with an atmosphere of legend; the Pythagorean school had raised credulity into a system. On all sides, and to a degree unparalleled in history, we find men . . . thirsting for belief, passionately and restlessly seeking for a new faith." W. E. H. Lecky, *History of European Morals* (London, 1911), p. 387.

In the closing years of the Republic and the early years of the Empire scepticism of the activities of oracles and soothsayers seems to have been more widespread. "[Cato] mirari se aiebat quod non rideret haruspex haruspicem cum vidisset"— [Cato] used to express his surprise that soothsayers did not laugh when meeting other soothsayers. Cicero, *De Divinatione*, ii, 51.

Recently, however, some writers have discussed both the tenuous bases and the lack of substantial intellectual content of the fashionable practice of forecasting; and they have also recognized clearly that the demand for these forecasts is often largely unrelated to their accuracy.[16] Some remarks by Mr. J. Hajnal of the University of Manchester (derived in part from an article by Professor E. Devons) apply very forcibly to the type of economic forecasting prominent in discussions on underdeveloped countries:

The main thing which stands out in my mind is a sort of paradox. An ever-increasing amount of forecasting is being done all over the world amid a growing scepticism about the accuracy of forecasts. . . .

Perhaps we should recognise that the demand for forecasts is generated in part by motives only weakly related to their accuracy; in other words that even very inaccurate forecasts fulfil a need. The point has been put in its sharpest form by Professor Devons when he compares the use of statistical forecasting as a guide for policy to the function of the magician in some primitive societies. For example, if you want to go out hunting and do not know whether the best hunting is to the north or to the south, you consult a magician; and that after all is a sensible thing to do because the important thing is to get

16. Notable critical contributions include A. D. Roy and C. F. Carter, *British Economic Statistics* (Cambridge, England, 1954); Ely Devons, "Statistics as a Basis for Policy," *Lloyds Bank Review*, No. 33 (July 1954), pp. 30-43; J. Hajnal, "Population Projections," *Journal of the Royal Statistical Society*, Vol. 118, Part I (1955), pp. 21-23.

Professor J. R. N. Stone in an article "The Fortune Teller," *Economica*, February 1943, was an early critic of certain types of statistical forecasts.

on with the hunting. It would be disastrous to get bogged down in arguing. Much the same need lies behind the demand sometimes faced by demographers "Give me some figures, any figures are better than none." What such people want, perhaps, is someone to make up their mind.[17]

A recurrent theme within the general field of economic development is the quest for a fundamental cause or causes of development, and in particular for reasons explaining why some countries were caught up in the stream of material progress sooner than were others. The attraction of this quest is hard to resist, and it directly and indirectly exercises wide influence. I was much attracted myself by this set of problems; in particular, I was fascinated by the factors behind the material stagnation of China. I now think that this may be largely a fruitless quest. Often, without realizing it, one is enmeshed in problems of causality, in problems of causes of causes, and in intractable problems of distinguishing between causes and effects, especially in the field of human attitudes and social institutions. This sort of quest may be as stifling to progress as was the quest for final causes in the natural sciences from Aristotle to the seventeenth century. Modern science began essentially when this quest was abandoned, to be replaced by observation of phenomena, particularly by attempts to ascertain results stemming from specified occurrences. Galileo's procedure in rolling balls of different sizes down inclined grooves probably seemed trivial to many of his contemporaries who were engaged in speculations on

17. *Loc. cit.*, pp. 21 and 23.

final causes, but it is a major landmark of human thought. Here are the comments on this by a distinguished British historian of science:

We need to cultivate the restraint of Galileo, who left the world of angels and spirits until the time should come when it could be explored, and contented himself with such principles as he could extract with confidence from experience, though the resolution committed him to such trivialities as the timing of balls rolling down grooves. It is that self-control—the voluntary restriction to the task of extending knowledge outwards from the observed to the unobserved instead of imposing imagined universal principles inwards on the world of observation—that is the essential hallmark of the man of science, distinguishing him most fundamentally from the non-scientific philosopher.[18]

I think students of the economics of underdeveloped countries would do well to ponder over this episode. You will appreciate that these remarks refer to speculation without observation, and in no way belittle the significance of theory and analysis, and even of creative imagination, in the framing of hypotheses, and perhaps also in the testing of their validity.

I must now return to the distinctions between positive economics, normative economics, and the art of political economy. The failure to draw these distinctions is, I think, one of the reasons for the unsatisfactory nature of much of the literature on underdeveloped countries. They bear especially on two

18. H. Dingle, *Monthly Notices of the Royal Astronomical Society*, 113 (London, 1953), p. 407.

topics of some practical and intellectual significance. The first is that of the effective performance of the functions of the economist in advising governments; the other is the relation between the propositions of economics and the political position of the economist. In both contexts the distinction is essential.

The economist can best serve the maker of policy by successful establishment of uniformities of behavior within his own sphere, which in turn makes possible in this sphere the prediction of the likely results of particular courses of action. But this function, although a necessary element in the rational framing of policy, is not a sufficient basis for a direct recommendation for policy. Direct recommendations for policy and decisions on policy must always be based on assessments of the political possibilities of different courses of action and of their probable results on the total social situation, among the many facets of which the economic is only one. Moreover, both recommendations for policy and measures of policy must be largely influenced by value judgments, especially by one's views on the kind of society one prefers.

The most effective and honest way in which the economist can contribute to policy is by stating the basis of his argument clearly and pursuing it rigorously within his own sphere, on the clear understanding that there are many other factors besides the economic which will be considered in the framing of policy. If the economist consistently pursues this course his competence in the performance of his duties can be assessed. Such an interpretation of the duties of the economist will also facilitate the task of the politician or administrator in allowing for other relevant considerations (that is, considerations outside the sphere of technical economics), and this in turn will make it easier to examine and assess their influence and relevance in particular circumstances.

If, however, the economist is preoccupied with direct policy recommendations, his propositions and conclusions will be much influenced by his assessment of the political possibilities of particular courses of action, as well as by value judgments and various other considerations which, although essentially relevant to the framing of policy, lie outside his technical competence. He thereby arrogates to himself the functions of the politician or civil servant whose special task it is to take into account these factors. The maker of policy, the politician or the civil servant, will then not know whether the economist has already taken these factors into account and has incorporated the necessary compromises into his analysis, or whether his conclusions reflect the results of technical analysis only. This then makes it impossible to assess the competence of the reasoning and of the analysis, and opens the field to the charlatans who can rationalize the faulty logic or the technical incompetence of their remarks by referring to the political problems or aims they allegedly had in mind. What is merely a failure in observation or analysis comes to be claimed as evidence of breadth of view, or of maturity of judgment, or of political wisdom.

Interest in economics generally, and in underdeveloped countries in particular, stems largely from concern with practical issues; the propositions even of positive economics generally have much bearing on policy. How far are the propositions of economics affected by our political position? I have already referred to the implications of the absence of contrived experiment, both for the establishment of economic generalizations and for their convincing presentation. The difficulties under both these headings, but especially in the problem of convincing presentation, are particularly acute in the economics of underdeveloped countries. In this sphere the evidence refers to conditions distant in space, and in a sense distant also in time, because the economic life of underdeveloped countries often corresponds to much earlier phases in the history of developed countries.

The propositions of positive economics which embody the results of the discernment of the uniformities behind the diversity of the events and phenomena of economic life are in principle independent of a political position. Their validity depends on their success in explaining and predicting phenomena— more especially in making successful predictions about particular phenomena not yet observed. In this fundamental sense a generalization is entirely unaffected by its political or psychological basis or background. This should be evident when we consider the simplest generalizations of economics, such as the inverse relationship between price and quantity demanded, a proposition the validity of which is obviously independent of a political position.[19] Yet in contemporary economic discussion, especially on underdeveloped countries, it is often suggested explicitly or by clear implication that the acceptance or even the acceptability or validity of economic propositions generally (without distinction between positive and normative statements) are largely matters of political position and thus of judgment, rather than a function of their usefulness and success in expressing, framing, or testing hypotheses which explain or predict phenomena.[20]

Much mischief has been caused in our subject by the failure to see that reference to its psychological or political background does not affect the validity (and thus the fundamental acceptability) of a generalization of positive economics. Such suggestions and attitudes really destroy the subject in the sense of a

19. In normative economics and in the art of political economy consideration of the political assumptions of propositions is in order, especially when specific proposals are under discussion. In assessing the merits of proposals it is legitimate to consider not only such assumptions but even personal and political motives. This is so for several reasons. For instance, the political position and the personal motives of the proponents of a measure may enable us to form a judgment of the probable distribution of the costs and benefits resulting from the measure. But such considerations differ from those discussed in the text, though the important differences and distinctions are often ignored. In the third lecture I shall suggest their relevance to wide issues of policy in the field of economic development, especially to proposals for taxation for development.

20. This is, for example, argued in some of the writings of Dr. Gunnar Myrdal, notably in *Development and Underdevelopment* (Cairo, 1956) and *An International Economy* (New York, 1956).

discipline of which the positive propositions at any rate embody the results of discernment of uniformities established by observation and analysis, which can be tested for consistency and for their power of explanation and prediction.

Generalizations which are simply functions of political opinion or of judgment will not command respect for long, within or outside economics. Such an outcome may be attractive in that it tends to prevent the emergence of an ossified othodoxy. But it does so at the cost of undermining the subject, the continued existence and progress of which, as those of any other discipline, postulate certain agreed minimum standards of technical competence. Without this agreement there can be no serious discussion. If everybody can have his say, then nobody can be heard, because serious argument is drowned in clamor, which differs from discussion in much the same way as does a mêlée from a boxing match. In a boxing match, the performance of the contestants can be assessed, and in a mêlée it cannot; therefore competent boxers command respect and participants in a mêlée do not.

These shortcomings are especially widespread and pervasive in economic discussion of underdeveloped countries, partly no doubt because of the comparatively recent resurgence of interest in that branch of economics, and also because of the important political and practical problems on which the economic study of underdeveloped countries bears. Preoccupation with practical issues, concern with pro-

motion of policy rather than with the promotion of
knowledge, has stood in the way of systematic work
in this branch of study, especially in the way of
careful collection and analysis of information designed to frame and test hypotheses, to establish the
width and limitations of generalizations. I think this
is one reason for the comparative paucity of illuminating observations and propositions which have
emerged so far from work in this field.

There is perhaps an interesting anomaly implicit
in this state of affairs. It is the practical relevance
of this branch of economic study which has elicited
the large sums of money for its pursuit. At the same
time, this concern with issues of policy has served to
retard the development of knowledge and the establishment of positive propositions which represent the
most appropriate and effective contribution of economics to the framing of policy.

Insistence on the independence of the propositions
of positive economics of political positions is not intended to dispute the fact that the interpretation of
phenomena is often difficult and complex; and that
the inferences drawn are often influenced by the ob-
server's political position. Nor is it intended to suggest that economic generalizations, even when unambiguously established, can serve as sufficient guide
to policy. I shall take these points in turn.

The response of supply and demand to changes in
price is a subject on which differences of opinion have
often arisen in the interpretation of phenomena. And
indeed this may present difficult problems. For in-

stance, the supply of a particular commodity is usually a positive function of price. This relationship stems ultimately from the limitation of resources which underlies the presence of costs, and the effects of which in bringing about a response of supply to price are reinforced by differences in the costs of different producers which in turn reflect differences in their circumstances. There may, however, be no easily observable statistical relationship between price and supply of, say, a particular agricultural product. Such absence of a readily observed response may reflect an absence of the usual positive response of supply to changes in price, for such reasons as the presence of effective barriers to entry, or the absence of money costs or of suitable alternative crops or activities open to producers, or lack of interest or of information. But an apparent lack of response of producers is compatible with a high response after some delay, or with a prompt response the manifestations of which are delayed (a familiar example of such a delayed manifestation is that stemming from the time-lag between the planting and maturity of trees in the production of commercial tree crops), or with a high response the effects of which are masked by the influence of extraneous factors. Detailed examination both of the conditions of production of the particular commodity and of the relevant statistics may be required to ascertain whether the absence of a readily observable response is likely to reflect an absence of the usual positive response of supply to price or whether it is more likely that the usual response operates but is not readily discernible. But the arguments and suggestions alleging the absence of a response of supply (or of demand) to price are frequently supported only by reference to the absence of an easily observable statistical relationship. Such reasoning usually reflects confusion between functional and historical relationships, which in turn reflects technical incompetence which may or may not be related to a particular political position. It does not reflect a genuine difficulty in the interpretation of phenomena, still less does it refute the elementary propositions of economics. The persistence of this type of confusion is an example of the difficulty of downing the unsuccessful hypothesis, to use Professor Friedman's expressive phrase.[21]

There is, however, a sense in which the study even of positive economics is much affected by a political position. This is in the choice of the topics selected for investigation. This particular influence of the political factor is not confined to economics, but applies to other disciplines also. Let me consider an

21. For instance, it is frequently alleged that the supply of smallholders' rubber varies inversely with price. In fact there is overwhelming detailed evidence to the contrary. The positive response to price of the supply of smallholders' rubber has also been recognized by the use of special export taxes under the various restriction schemes designed to restrict the export of smallholders' rubber by depressing the local price. This method both presupposes and recognizes the positive response of the supply of smallholders' rubber to price.

Again it has often been argued that the extremely heavy export taxes on West African crops have not affected output, a suggestion advanced without reference to evidence, or with reference to evidence which can only relate to confusion of historical and functional relationships.

analogy from another field, that of biology. There are large numbers of people who hold religious beliefs incompatible with the principal generalizations of evolutionary biology. Such people, whose numbers may exceed those who accept the theory of evolution, will not usually pursue this branch of knowledge. It is thus perfectly correct to say that those who do engage in this study have preconceived notions, and that in this sense both the subject and the results of their study are influenced by their position. But this does not affect the scientific validity of their generalizations, which depends on the success of these generalizations in explaining and predicting phenomena. The same reasoning applies to the propositions of economics.

Of course, even if an economic generalization has been successfully established and its applicability to particular conditions is agreed, it is not by itself sufficient basis for policy. Even if there is general agreement that the supply of a particular product responds positively and substantially to the price received by the producers, it may still be argued that it should be heavily taxed on various grounds of policy. Thus, although the conclusions of positive economics are necessary for a rational framing of policy, they are not sufficient for the purpose. This is a matter to which I shall revert in the third lecture.

Failure to distinguish between positive economics, normative economics and the art of political economy, and especially between normative and positive propositions, and neglect of elementary standards of technical competence, which in turn stems in part from the failure to observe these distinctions, exposes economics to great danger. Within economics, it encourages intellectual sloth because lack of sustained reasoning can be rationalized plausibly but speciously as evidence of political wisdom. Such developments and attitudes are likely to affect the intellectual carriage and stature of economists, and are also likely to undermine their self-respect, which in turn is likely to be folllowed by a loss of the respect of others.

I know that this sounds paradoxical at a time when the services of the economist are in greater demand than ever before, and the prestige of the subject is very high. The paradox is only apparent. I have suggested elsewhere that the standing of economics may be too high and its standards may be too low. This discrepancy or weakness bears on the prospects of the subject. The fundamental position and prospects of a discipline, or of an organization, or of an institution, cannot be inferred from their prestige at a particular time. There is much historical evidence to suggest that the prestige of a subject, as of an institution, can be high, and yet its prospects may be poor.

I must not delve further into problems of method, but must proceed to consider some economic aspects of the underdeveloped world. This discussion on method will, however, bear on some of the argument of my next two lectures.

2

Some Features of the Economic Landscape

> Compare the cultivation of the lands in the neighbourhood of any considerable town with that of those which lie at some distance from it, and you will easily satisfy yourself how much the country is benefited by the commerce of the town. ADAM SMITH

> We must not picture to ourselves an unreal world as it might, or ought to be, and make schemes for it. That way lies social madness, leading to a failure of hot aspirations and thence to cold reaction. Our first duty as economists is to make a reasoned catalogue of the world as it is. . . . ALFRED MARSHALL

IN THIS LECTURE I shall discuss a few aspects of the economies of underdeveloped countries, especially in the Commonwealth. Even at the risk of laboring the obvious, I must remind you that I can deal with but a very few of the salient aspects of these economies; and there is always the danger that a discussion intended to illuminate part of the landscape, and especially only a small part of it, may plunge the surrounding area into greater darkness. In these circumstances the process of selection is not an easy one; a leading modern historian has reminded us that the more selective the art, the greater the art of selection.

I have chosen the topics largely with an eye to the relevance of economics: that is, they are salient features of the landscape, the configuration of which may be better understood with the help of economics and which in turn offer a fruitful field for economic enquiry; but, again they are only a small part of the field to which economics is relevant.[1] I believe that these topics also bear on economic development in many underdeveloped countries. There may well be other aspects and activities which affect development much more, especially in the institutional and technical field, but as an economist I have not much to say on them, particularly within the compass of one brief lecture.

The underdeveloped world today is often implicitly and even explicitly compared to the western world on the eve of the industrial revolution. This is most misleading. As a result of slow but prolonged economic and technical progress, western Europe had reached by the seventeenth and eighteenth centuries a high level of economic and technical attainment, far

1. Even such important and relevant features of the landscape as the extended family, the unemployment stemming from lack of co-operant resources, and the narrowness of markets are wholly or largely ignored in the discussion. They are reviewed in the Cambridge Economic Handbook already mentioned.

higher than that reached by many underdeveloped countries by the beginning of the twentieth century, or in many cases even at present.[2]

Bacon, Descartes, Galileo, Harvey thought and wrote more than a century, and Newton and Leibniz more than half a century, before the date conventionally ascribed to the beginning of the industrial revolution. Tables of logarithms were published at the beginning of the seventeenth century; the Royal Society was founded in 1662. The widespread and pervasive intellectual curiosity, sustained effort, and spirit of experimentation in science, industry, and agriculture are obvious from the general literature and the scientific publications of the seventeenth and eighteenth centuries, and in the eighteenth century they are also reflected in newspapers and periodicals. The economic and technical achievements are also manifest in such technical achievements as the buildings and ships of the period, or perhaps more characteristically, in such instruments as clocks, telescopes, and microscopes. These faculties are also reflected in the volume and direction of travel, almost all of which was from Europe and America to Africa and Asia with practically no reverse movement.

The political and social institutions in England and western Europe in the eighteenth century, which had evolved through the long period of progress

2. Much of the argument of the next few paragraphs does not apply to Latin America, especially South America, chiefly because it is an area of recent settlement and a large proportion of the population is of European stock, that is, the migrants came from comparatively highly developed countries.

since the tenth century, conduced greatly both to the spirit of experimentation and to the taking of long views in economic decisions. There were highly developed banking systems and some advanced money markets in these countries, and there was a general expectation that private contracts would be honored.

In short, by the eighteenth century Great Britain and western Europe had had centuries of sustained development behind them, had reached a high degree of cultural, technical, and economic achievement. Perhaps even more important, they had become almost completely pervaded by an exchange economy. In these respects, as was frequently noted at the time, they were already far ahead of other countries.

Compare this with the position of the underdeveloped countries today, or a few decades ago. Africa south of the Sahara has never invented the wheel; over large parts of Africa, including West Africa, even fifty years ago most people had never seen one. There was still cannibalism in West Africa towards the end of the last century, and slavery was a recognized institution until well into this century. The position and development of most of the indigenous peoples of Africa and Southeast Asia at the beginning of this century resembled not that of the West in the seventeenth and eighteenth centuries, but, at best, those of northern and western Europe in the sixth and seventh centuries, when the Germanic tribes of these regions were first visited by Christian missionaries.

Large parts of Asia and of the Middle East were in a rather different position in that in the past they had enjoyed high cultural and technical standards and were the repositories of a great cultural heritage. But the technical achievements had very largely disappeared—or had been submerged—by the eighteenth century. Even where the cultural heritage survived, the technical and economic achievement was meager, and the social institutions were very uncongenial to economic development. As late as the end of the nineteenth century the level of economic and technical achievement and the general social and political conditions in these areas were far less conducive to material progress than had been those of Great Britain and western Europe in the eighteenth century.

I do not suggest, of course, that these countries will require a millennium to reach the position of eighteenth-century Europe. Nor, I hope, will anyone infer from my remarks that their populations cannot reach the cultural and technical achievements of the West. The frequent changes, even within comparatively short historical periods, in the economic and cultural leadership, and even in the standard of living and in technical and economic performance, of the different nations should warn us against any such idea. And equally they should caution us against a ready acceptance of the idea of a necessary cumulative tendency towards ever-widening inequalities in these respects between countries. Differences in performance do not seem to reflect inevitably fixed inherent biological differences. For instance, until a few years ago not only had the Africans not invented the wheel, but they had failed to introduce it even when it was brought to their notice, as it often was. By now, however, they are accepting it avidly.

Although the level of economic attainment in the underdeveloped world is generally still low this does not mean that these countries are generally stagnant. Poverty is compatible with even very rapid growth, if the growth is of recent origin, and the country in question had until recently reached only a very low level of technical and economic attainment. This is, in fact, the position in many underdeveloped countries in which the economy, or at least substantial sectors of it, are growing very rapidly but in which incomes are still low because the economy has only recently started on the road of material progress. It seems that much current discussion confuses levels of income and output with rate of change, perhaps taking for granted that the former are so low in underdeveloped countries that they could hardly have been significantly lower in the past.

This very rapid development has been particularly obvious in parts of Africa and Southeast Asia. Consistently compiled national income figures would, of course, provide the most comprehensive statistical indices of the growth which has taken place, although for reasons which I shall discuss shortly even these would not convey adequately the changes which have taken place. But in fact there are no series of national income figures for any country in these regions going back even to so recent a period as that before the Second World War. At present the national income as conventionally measured is about £100 per head in Malaya, about £50 per head in the Gold Coast, and about £25 per head in Nigeria. These are low figures by western standards, but they still represent substantial advances over the last fifty years or so. At the beginning of this century these countries had barely progressed from subsistence economies to emerging exchange economies.

But although we have no series of national income figures, there is ample evidence of rapid economic growth in these areas over the last half century. The most easily accessible figures are, of course, statistics of foreign trade. Although these refer to a particular sector only, they are nevertheless of interest in those economies in which foreign trade is a significant part of the national income; in which exports are produced by members of the local population and the bulk of imports is destined for their use; and in which the decision to produce for export is a voluntary one on the part of producers, and not the result of central direction (or of compulsion by means of taxation forcing the population to earn incomes to pay the taxes). British West Africa and Malaya are examples of such economies.

In West Africa at the turn of the century there were practically no exports of such staple products as cocoa from the Gold Coast, or of cocoa, groundnuts, or cotton from Nigeria; the exports of palm-oil and palm-kernels from Nigeria were at that time about one-tenth of their present volume. In both Nigeria and the Gold Coast the annual values of both imports and exports were then about £1 million, against £100 million today; as prices have approximately quintupled over the period, there has been an approximately twenty-fold increase in volume. Malaya presents another convenient example of rapid economic development over the last half century. In 1900 there were no exports of plantation rubber from Malaya. By the 1930's there were about a half million tons a year, about half of which was then produced by smallholders. Much related information is available to confirm the general picture of growth in these countries. There has been a great increase in the volume, range and variety of imports, and in the consumption of excisable goods, both in total and per head. There has also been a substantial increase in agricultural production for local consumption, obviously in total, and almost certainly per head. This is suggested by such information as railway returns, occasional crop and acreage figures, sales of fishing and agricultural equipment, and the like. Statistics of government revenue and of public health again confirm the picture.

Africa and Southeast Asia offer the most striking examples of rapid growth among underdeveloped countries in the Commonwealth. Indeed, a book on West Africa published in the 1920's is very appropriately entitled *The Economic Revolution in Brit-*

ish West Africa.[3]   Even in India, where economic
progress in recent decades has been slower than
in many other underdeveloped countries, there is
much evidence of economic progress from such information as the volume of industrial production,
the increase in the literacy rate, the reduction in
famine and disease, the fall in the infant mortality
rate, the increased consumption of fresh fruit and
vegetables, and the substitution of higher for lower
quality food grains.

The kind of information to which I have referred
does not adequately describe the profound changes
which have taken place over the last half-century in
Southeast Asia, West Africa and in many other underdeveloped regions.   Malaya, which in the 1890's was
a sparsely populated country of Malay hamlets and
fishing villages, has been completely transformed by
the rise of the rubber industry, and has developed into a country with populous cities, thriving commerce,
and an excellent system of roads.   In West Africa
slave raiding and slavery (which frequently entailed
castration) were still widespread at the end of the
nineteenth century; in 1900 the towns of northern Nigeria, which are now centers of the groundnut trade,
were important slave markets.

Such profound changes in the conditions of life
greatly reduce the meaningfulness of discussions as to
whether the differences in real income per head between these countries and some more developed areas
have widened or narrowed over the last half century.

3. By A. McPhee (London, 1926).

In particular I doubt whether the concept of income, conventionally measured, is helpful in indicating or expressing them.

The inadequacy of the conventional national income estimates for conveying such far-reaching changes is reinforced by certain implications of the increase in population which has accompanied economic growth in these and in many other countries. For instance, the population of Malaya, in 1890 about one and a half million, is today about seven million; the number of Malays has risen from about one million or almost certainly less to over three million. Economic progress is usually measured by the growth of real income per head. This procedure implies an important value judgment which is generally covert and unrecognized. The increase in population in underdeveloped countries is brought about by the fall in the death rate (especially, but not only, among children) and this implies a longer expectation of life. Thus there is here an obvious and real psychic income. Its reality is clear from people's readiness to pay for the satisfaction of the postponement of death. Thus the usual way of drawing conclusions from income per head obscures important conceptual problems of the defined and measured income. It also implies a judgment that a high birth rate is a sign of an inability rather than of an unwillingness to control birth. Quite clearly, reliance on the conventionally measured income per head as a criterion of progress at times obscures the improvement in the economic position of individuals, besides understating the growth which has taken place.[4]

These considerations, especially those relating to the reduction in death rates, are germane to international comparisons in terms of income per head, when economic advance is accompanied by a more rapid increase in population in underdeveloped countries than in advanced countries. Because of this change in the relative numbers in different countries, the mean income per head may fall in the world as a whole, or even perhaps within the underdeveloped world, even if it has increased in every single country, poor or rich. Moreover, an improvement in real income per head throughout the underdeveloped world may be accompanied by an increase in the international inequality of incomes conventionally measured; for instance, there may be an increase in the proportion of people with incomes below the mean. There may even be a fall in the mean income in the world as a whole or within the underdeveloped world even if in all countries the mean income has risen—a familiar statistical result of a change in the relative importance of the component elements of an aggregate.

The impact of development on an economy invariably affects first particular activities and areas and

4. Conversely, the transfer of economic activity from the subsistence sector to the exchange sector may have the opposite effect, that is, to overstate the increase in incomes that has taken place.

There are many other conceptual and statistical problems in the compilation, comparison, and interpretation of national income figures in underdeveloped countries. References to discussions of this problem will be found in the list of readings at the end of this book.

from these spreads to the rest of the economy by a process which necessarily takes time. The need to develop resources and to adjust institutions alone ensures that appreciable time is normally required for this process. Thus, in all economies which do not stagnate completely, some sectors or areas will be more advanced and will be advancing more rapidly than others. This is familiar from the history of all developed countries and is so in the underdeveloped countries at the present time.

In the underdeveloped countries the advanced or advancing sectors are those in contact with personnel, ideas, and capital from more advanced economies. The differences in technical achievements between the developed countries and the underdeveloped countries are almost certainly wider than they were before the eighteenth century, while physical communications between them are certainly easier; moreover, the underdeveloped countries started on the road to economic development in recent decades from a technically and culturally very low level. Thus differences between the more and less advanced regions and sectors in underdeveloped countries may be wider, and are certainly more noticeable, than were similar differences in the earlier history of the developed countries. In many underdeveloped countries the impact of development in certain sectors has been sudden and the economic advance in these has been very rapid. This has resulted in marked differences and contrasts between different parts of the economy, often amounting to an anachronistic coexistence of the very old and the very new.

Some of the large Indian cities are huge centers of industry and commerce, while the mass of the population lives in villages the physical appearance and mode of life of which have changed little over centuries, except that they are now much less frequented by famine or epidemic disease. The physical appearance of the streets in the towns also reflects these contrasts; the bustling traffic is interrupted by cattle walking about or lying in the streets. The narrow streets of many towns of the Middle East seem to be just wide enough to accommodate a truck or a large American car. You stand close against the wall to avoid these instruments of modern life—but you also have to be careful to avoid the camel which may follow them.

These physical contrasts are obvious to the eye. Other contrasts are less obvious but probably more important. In Port Harcourt, a busy trading center in eastern Nigeria, there are a number of African traders, mainly women, operating on a very large scale. In 1950 the turnover of one of these traders with one of the large European merchant firms in the town amounted to several hundred thousand pounds. Yet thirty miles from Port Harcourt there were then villages in which the sale of meat without the hide was prohibited, to make sure than no human flesh was sold for consumption. Sometimes the contrasts are merged in one person. Thus the Oni of Ife, the leading African chief in western Nigeria, is a director of large commercial undertakings; in his capacity as spiritual head of the Yoruban nation he is considered responsible for regulating the supply of rainfall in western Nigeria.

These contrasts often make it difficult to find one's bearings in the economic and social landscape of the underdeveloped world. I think they have misled those observers who have suggested that these advanced sectors and forms of economic activity are simply outposts of developed economies, enclaves owned and operated from abroad, which contribute little to the economic development of these countries and of their populations.

In fact, however, large sectors of these advanced types of economic activity are owned and administered by members of the local population, and much or most of the income generated there accrues to them. These cities, regions, and activities are essentially the focal points or centers of development, which necessarily starts in particular areas and activities. Differences in the rate of progress of different sectors of an economy, and notably the presence of backward sectors, do not imply that the development which has taken place cannot or will not pervade the rest of the economy. As I have already said, differences in economic achievement and in the rate of development are very general in advancing economies; for instance, they are, and have always been, conspicuous in the United States. The rate at which development pervades the rest of the economy depends, among other things, on institutional and physical factors, on restrictions to movement, and on the economic attitudes of different sections of the population.

In the economic advance which has taken place in underdeveloped countries the role of agricultural production for sale both locally and for export has been prominent. This is hardly surprising. The skills and other resources of the population have for centuries been geared to agriculture, which, together with its ancillary activities, is much the most important economic activity in the subsistence stage. Production for export has been specially significant in initiating economic development. It has drawn these countries into a wider system of exchange; it has also provided the basis of government revenues, which in turn made possible the more extended provision of government services and the construction and expansion of basic communications. Although the initiative often came from abroad, the response of the local population has been striking. The principal export crops of West Africa are produced on millions of small properties established, owned, and operated by Africans. About two-thirds of world exports of natural rubber come from Asian-owned properties, mostly from quite small holdings owned and operated by Malaysians and Chinese.

The emergence and spread of the production of these crops are a response to opportunities presented by the provision of a market, a facet of greater accessibility. Establishment of settled government, suppression of tribal warfare, arrival of administrators and traders, establishment and improvement of communications and of transport and storage facilities—these influences have created, or have greatly widened, the contacts with more advanced economies. As a result of these influences, areas which had been inaccessible became accessible in the economic sense of the term in that it became possible there to produce commodities the costs of production and transport of which were less than the market prices.

The key role of accessibility in economic production and development is very clearly reflected in the establishment and growth of these cash crops in the Commonwealth. The rubber tree is not indigenous in Malaya, and the soil of the country is indifferent. At the turn of the century Malaya had practically no indigenous wage-earning labor force and no local supply of capital. Yet within a few years a large rubber industry grew up, because market conditions became favorable, and the country had access to technical and administrative skill and to supplies of labor and capital. No one surveying the economic position and prospects of Malaya in 1890 could have foreseen that within a few years this would be a thriving country and the largest producer of natural rubber. Much the same applies to West African cocoa and groundnuts, to Uganda cotton, and to several other important cash crops in the Commonwealth.

Before I turn to my next topic I should like to clear up a possible misunderstanding, or rather to forestall a possible objection. The insistence on the development which has taken place should not be taken as a suggestion that all is for the best in these countries, or for a plea for *laissez faire*, or any other particular policy. What I have to say in these lectures on the role of government in underdeveloped countries belongs to the next lecture. But it is obvious that the problems of rapid and uneven growth are quite different from those of stagnation, and will call for a very different kind of official action. And the growth which has taken place is amply sufficient to dispose of the suggestion that these countries stagnate, or are otherwise caught in a vicious circle of poverty.

Production of cash crops has been generally accompanied by the establishment, extension, and improvement of agricultural properties, that is by fixed capital formation in agriculture. This important aspect of the economic landscape has been much neglected in contemporary literature, in which significant categories of capital and capital formation are often ignored. Cultivated agricultural properties and their extension and improvement are the most important of these neglected categories; others are livestock, various types of equipment, simple structures, and, in a related field, traders' inventories.[5]

In underdeveloped countries agriculture and its ancillary activities are a large proportion of economic activity. Whether they are used for the production

5. Most of my remarks in this context apply to capital both as a stock and as a flow. Where the reference is only to the one concept or to the other, this will either be clear from the context or will be indicated appropriately.

of subsistence crops or cash crops, cultivated agricultural properties are income-yielding assets, the
productivity of which exceeds that of unimproved
land as a result of the expenditure of human effort
and activity; and the process of establishing, extending, and improving the land is investment. To disregard it amounts to neglecting all direct agricultural
investment in the non-monetary sector of the economy, as well as much of it in the monetary sector
(when the land is used for the production of cash
crops).[6]

There may be various reasons for the neglect in
the literature of these categories of capital and
capital formation. An unsympathetic attitude to agriculture and a tendency to underrate its role in economic development may have played a part. An inclination to confine attention largely to easily meas-
urable economic categories may be another reason.
Estimates of these types of capital present formidable
problems of concept and measurement. But this does
not justify their neglect. The reality and significance
of a concept or phenomenon are not commensurate
with the ease with which they can be quantified. But
the oversight is almost certainly also connected with
an implicit belief or assumption of much current discussion, namely that over most of the economy the
exchange economy is already fully developed, or at
any rate that the factors affecting its extension are not

6. The argument is not affected by the fact that at times production for sale is in substitution for subsistence production. The
establishment and spread of cash crops presupposes the establishment and improvement of agricultural properties.

a concern of economic discussion or policy. Such a treatment is obviously inappropriate to underdeveloped countries. It is a characteristic of these countries that large parts of their economies have not yet been pervaded by a money or exchange economy, and that over large areas there is little or no production for sale beyond restricted local markets. The extension of the exchange economy is generally an essential condition of economic development.

The neglect of these types of investment has resulted in anomalies. Thus the expenditure of about £35 million on the East African groundnut scheme is regarded as investment, though it has not produced any groundnuts; yet the establishment and improvement of hundreds of thousands of agricultural properties, producing in the aggregate a huge tonnage, is generally disregarded in discussions and estimates of capital formation. The establishment and improvement of rubber estates is regarded as investment, but that of smallholdings is usually not so treated. More generally, the incomplete estimates of investment (that is, estimates which refer only to part of total investment) are frequently related to the total population, or to the total national income, with misleading results. Moreover, the neglected categories are also qualitatively important in the sense that they play an important part in the development from subsistence production to a market economy. The presence and importance of the neglected categories of capital qualify but do not invalidate the general conclusion that the level of capital in underdeveloped countries is generally very low compared to more advanced economies. This is indeed a characteristic of underdeveloped countries. But the oversight has important implications both for description and analysis of these economies, and also for wide issues of policy, as I shall suggest in the last lecture.

The presence of these types of capital investment bears on the influential proposition that the underdeveloped countries are too poor to invest as they have no surplus above subsistence, and that they are thereby caught in a vicious circle of poverty.[7] Although there is an element of truth in this argument, in its unqualified form (in which it is usually presented) it is open to about half-a-dozen different objections. The most obvious objection is that if this argument were valid it is difficult to see how the developed countries could have reached their present position, since all developed countries began by being underdeveloped. The substantial capital formation in agriculture evidenced by the rapid growth of cash crops in underdeveloped countries is a further refutation of the thesis of the vicious circle of underdevelopment.

The advance from subsistence production by means of the cultivation of cash crops and investment in agriculture bears also on the ingenious hypothesis

7. To quote a typical formulation of this argument: "They [the backward nations] cannot get their heads above water because their production is so low that they can spare nothing for capital formation by which their standard of living could be raised." Paul A. Samuelson, *Economics: An Introductory Analysis* (2nd edition, New York, 1951), p. 49.

advanced by Professor Nurkse that contact with advanced economies is damaging to underdeveloped countries by raising the propensity to consume, thus discouraging saving and preventing investment. To quote:

Knowledge of or contact with new consumption patterns opens one's eyes to previously unrecognised possibilities. . . . In the poorer countries such goods are often imported goods, not produced at home; but that is not the only trouble. The basic trouble is that the presence or the mere knowledge of new goods and new methods of consumption tends to raise the general propensity to consume.[8]

The vicious circle that keeps down the domestic supply of capital in low-income areas is bad enough by itself. My point is that it tends to be made even worse by the stresses that arise from relative as distinct from absolute poverty. How much worse is a question that cannot be precisely determined; it is a matter of judgment and one that presumably varies from country to country.[9]

Professor Nurkse's hypothesis has come to be known as the international demonstration effect. It will be noted that although Professor Nurkse regards this effect as a further obstacle to capital formation and thus to economic development (in a sense substituting another vicious circle of poverty and underdevelopment if the first vicious circle has been broken through), he adds that the strength of this effect and

8. *Problems of Capital Formation in Underdeveloped Countries* (Oxford 1953), pp. 61-62.
9. *Ibid.*, p. 70.

its applicability to different countries are matters of judgment. Unfortunately it is the more uncompromising version of his proposition which has come to be most widely quoted. Yet without substantial qualifications, the international demonstration effect and, more generally, the suggested adverse effect of contact with more developed countries, cannot be accepted as significant obstacles to capital formation and to development of underdeveloped countries.

Indeed, the effects of contact with more advanced countries are usually very different from those assumed by the international demonstration effect. It almost invariably accelerates economic growth in less developed countries by encouraging production for the market, by suggesting new wants, new crops, and improved methods generally. This indeed is a commonplace of economic history. And at present throughout the underdeveloped world the more advanced sectors and areas are those which are in contact with the more developed countries.

The usual formulation of the international demonstration effect omits to note that the new types of consumer goods can be bought only if incomes are first earned to purchase them; and that the desire for higher consumption can stimulate saving and investment as a means to such consumption. Indeed, until quite recently the absence of new wants and the inelasticity of consumption and of standards of living were regarded as major obstacles to economic development. Investment is very generally necessary to make possible production for sale, which in turn is necessary to secure the incomes required for the purchase of the desired consumer goods. In these circumstances the demonstration effect resulting from contact with more developed economies induces a higher economic performance; this influence is reinforced because the contact usually not only suggests new wants but also acquaints the population with new crops and methods of production, the adoption of which makes possible the satisfaction of the new wants. Moreover, by generating cash incomes this process also promotes investment in other parts of the economy: public investment made possible by increased revenues is only one obvious example. The usual exposition of the international demonstration effect seems to assume that the exchange economy has already permeated the entire economy, or at any rate that the supply of effort to the exchange sector and its rate of expansion are not affected by the attractiveness of the rewards obtainable in that sector. These are assumptions which are inapplicable to most underdeveloped countries.

There is, however, an important area of economic life in which the international demonstration effect does seem to operate, though in a manner rather different from that proposed in its usual exposition. Governments, politicians, and public servants in underdeveloped countries seem to be very susceptible to it in adopting or seeking to adopt technical, educational, and social standards which are inappropriate and wasteful. The same applies to the attraction of conspicuous and spectacular investment and of elaborate and spectacular schemes, often using expensive equipment demanding high skills. Such acts of economic showmanship are a feature of contemporary life, and they are not confined to public authorities nor to underdeveloped countries. But they have been especially conspicuous in the public sector of many of these countries. Nor is this surprising. The governments and public servants in these countries are being pressed to rival the standards of developed countries. Readiness to yield to these pressures may be a condition of political survival; and in yielding to these pressures the politicians and the administrators do not spend their own resources.

In many underdeveloped countries there is a large volume of trading activity. Production for sale by large numbers of farmers, each operating on a small scale, is the principal factor behind this feature of the economy. The farmers generally produce on a small scale, and as they have little storage capacity and small cash resources they have to sell in small lots at frequent intervals. Usually many, or most, producers are far from the points of assembly, the principal markets or the ports of shipment. The cost of assembling and conveying to the market, often over long distances, a large number of small parcels of produce is heavy. For instance, Nigerian groundnuts are produced by hundreds of thousands of farmers and the saleable annual output of the great majority is less than one-half ton. The producers operate about eight hundred to a thousand miles from the ports, and often hundreds of miles from the railhead. The reverse side of the same task is that of the distribution of consumer goods to a large number of widely dispersed buyers who have low incomes and cash reserves and small storage facilities. Again, many of the buyers are far from the ports or the principal markets. They may want to buy, or indeed may have to buy, in very small quantities—three lumps of sugar, half a cigarette, individual drops of perfume, a few sticks of matches, all of which are common units of retail purchase in Nigeria; these are the last stages of a distributive chain which often begins with the import of merchandise in individual consignments of hundreds of tons or cases.

Thus the distributive task of raising and maintaining the economy above subsistence level absorbs a large volume of resources. The type of resource used will depend on the relative supplies and prices of capital and labor, on technical conditions, and on institutional factors. Compared to conditions in advanced countries, capital in these countries is generally scarce in proportion to unskilled labor; small-scale distribution, especially trade and transport, requires little capital and training; most intermediaries are themselves poor, so that they can handle only a small volume; the lack of telephones and the poor quality of the roads increase the capital required for a given flow of consumption and production; and institutional factors, including restrictions on the access to land, and the establishment of institutionally fixed wage rates for hired labor in large-scale or medium-scale industry and commerce forces many people to fall back on petty trade and transport. These factors explain why distribution not only absorbs a large volume of resources in many underdeveloped countries, but is also often labor intensive.

Little of this emerges from the occupational statistics, chiefly because in these countries specialization is incomplete, and most of the small-scale traders are also agriculturists or their dependents; indeed, it is often impossible to distinguish between agriculture and distribution when the farmer or members of his family sell or exchange the produce. However, the presence of much trading activity is suggested by such information as transport statistics, which show large-scale movement of crops; the proportion of the population living in towns; the variety and volume of foodstuffs on sale in markets, often from distant parts of the country; the presence of thousands of stalls in the large markets, apart from the petty traders and hawkers operating both there and in the streets at large; and the activity on the roads, paths, and rivers in the transport of crops and merchandise by man, beast, and machine.

This large volume of distributive activity is necessary for emergence from subsistence production. It serves to widen markets, to bring new commodities to the notice of and within the reach of actual or prospective producers, whom it also acquaints with new methods and crops. In these and other ways it lifts and maintains the economy above subsistence production, and conduces both to the more economic utilization of existing resources and to the encouragement of their growth. I shall not labor these obvious general considerations, nor discuss possible exceptions of small practical significance in underdeveloped countries.[10]

I want, however, to mention one or two important aspects of trading activity which at times go unobserved. First, there is the special role of the traders in promoting the emergence of the exchange economy in outlying areas. This part is often played by itinerant vendors, or occupiers of small shacks, possibly many miles from any substantial town. Their small stock of merchandise may induce subsistence producers to begin producing for sale; the traders also often bring to their notice new crops and methods to enable them to do so. To be successful these traders must be able to survive on a low income, and must possess endurance and thrift. They also need some commercial imagination to gauge correctly the wants, requirements, and potentialities of the prospective customers. This type of trade is often risky, both because of the large physical distances and the slow turnover of stock, and because of the uncertainty of

10. Resale price maintenance, which in developed countries is often responsible for additional distributive activity, is of very little practical significance in underdeveloped countries. Few articles of commerce are covered by it in these countries, and also it is practically always ineffective. Customary price or the operation of price rings are of somewhat greater importance, but in the absence of contrived barriers to entry they also are rarely effective for long; cf. also my book *West African Trade* (Cambridge, 1954), *passim*, esp. chap. xviii.

the response of the population. It is a combination of the ability to survive on a low income and the possession of considerable commercial abilities (at any rate commercial abilities much greater than those currently displayed by the indigenous population) which explains the prominence of Chinese, Indians, and Levantines in this field.

My second point refers to two distinctions or contrasts, one between traders and agriculturalists, and the other between traders and industrialists. These contrasts are frequently drawn much too sharply to fit the facts of underdeveloped countries. The indigenous traders are often also farmers, and very generally members of farming families. But they are often the more ambitious and resourceful members of their community. The contrast between traders and industrialists is often also blurred, as traders quite often turn to industry, transport, or estate agriculture when the economy has advanced, or when they have become more experienced and have accumulated capital. This familiar phenomenon of economic history is at present observable in many underdeveloped countries. In India and Malaya a large proportion of successful industrial and plantation enterprises have been established by merchants. This is most obvious in the activities of foreign-owned enterprises, but it is equally true of successful indigenous industrialists. In West Africa, for instance, almost all successful African industrial enterpreneurs or transport contractors are, or have been, traders or their employees. This is not surprising, since such experience acquaints people with the working of a money economy, and especially with the habitual and orderly management of business affairs, besides providing contacts and a knowledge of the market.[11]

Most of what I have said about the work of traders applies to them irrespective of their nationality. But, as is well known, foreigners and migrants have played a disproportionate role in the economic life of many countries—I hardly need emphasize this in America. At present, in spite of severe restrictions on their activities, the part played by European, Chinese, Indian, and Lebanese migrants is still conspicuous in the underdeveloped world.

The disproportionate contribution of migrants to the economic life of their adopted countries and the principal reasons for it are well known. The tendency of migrants to proceed where their skills and aptitudes are most valuable; the stimulating effect of the change in environment; the familiarity with different methods and products, and the inclination to question, compare, and experiment; the comparative freedom from social and customary bonds; the probability that emigrants are a self-selected sample of the more able and enterprising members of the population; the social cohesion of migrants; their exclusion from important categories of noncommercial activities—these

11. This obvious, though often neglected, consideration is no new discovery: "The habits besides of order, economy, and attention, to which mercantile business naturally forms a merchant, render him much fitter to execute, with profit and success, any project of improvement." *Wealth of Nations,* Book III, chap iv.

are among the more obvious factors. They may help to explain, for example, the remarkable contribution which the Chinese migrants, who came from backward and poor regions of their homeland, have made to the economic development of Malaya. The Chinese in China had failed to contribute to the development of their native provinces, and so had the Malays in Malaya; but the Chinese in Malaya have made a great contribution.

I shall refer to one or two special aspects only of this wide subject. Even when the migrants have entered the country without capital, they have, in the aggregate, often created capital on a massive scale by spending less than their incomes. Once again this is obvious from American economic history. This type or category of capital formation is often overlooked, both in discussions on underdeveloped countries and in the framing of policy, since it represents neither capital imports nor the fruits of saving by the indigenous population. It is likely to be particularly productive, because it rarely takes the form of conspicuous investment and other forms of economic showmanship; it is generally invested and managed by those who have accumulated it. This form of capital formation serves as yet another refutation of the idea of the vicious circle of poverty allegedly set up by a low level of income. Quite apart from numerous other historical examples, the results of the substantial capital formation by penniless Chinese immigrants in Malaya, by the often very poor Indian migrants in East Africa, by Levantines in West Africa and Brazil, and by Jews in South Africa, are at present conspicuous in these regions and countries.[12]

Besides any contribution to the supply of capital, migrants often also contribute skills not available locally, or at any rate available only at a higher real cost. In this way too their presence serves to relieve the unemployment stemming from the lack of co-operant factors which is often a feature of underdeveloped countries. Once in a country, they can contribute most effectively to the economy if they can move between activities, particularly from trade into industry, and they are much more likely to succeed in industry if they have previously acted as traders.[13]

There are manifest and striking differences between racial and ethnic groups in such qualities as industry, thrift, enterprise, and the readiness to perceive and exploit economic opportunity, and there are resulting differences in economic performance. The Chinese in Malaya, the Indians in East Africa, the Lebanese in West Africa—usually migrants without capital and without much formal education—have quite soon greatly surpassed the economic performance of the indigenous population. I doubt whether the special conditions of migrants completely account for these

12. Immigrants also make demands on the capital resources of the economy in various ways and in different degrees. This is a consideration which is generally relevant to the framing and administration of immigration policy but which does not affect the discussion in the text.

13. The discussion in the text does not, of course, provide conclusive argument in favor of large-scale unrestricted immigration. As will be noted in the next lecture the desirability of such a policy cannot be assessed on economic grounds alone.

great differences in economic quality and performance. I do not know the historical or biological factors behind racial differences in economic performance. It seems probable that climatic and other environmental factors play an important part, and also that the differences are not fixed for all time. This last point is suggested by the frequent changes in industry and commercial leadership between nations, and also by the evident differences in the responses of the same ethnic groups to ideas and opportunities at different times. However, at any given time, or over a period of years or even decades, the differences in the economic qualities and attitudes between races and individuals are pronounced and important.

In a subsistence economy these differences are largely irrelevant. But they come into play when the economy emerges from this stage, and this can be observed in many underdeveloped countries. Here is an example from Nigeria. In northern Nigeria there is a Hausa trader operating on a large scale. He had spent his childhood in the Gold Coast around the turn of the century. As a young man he become a cattle trader, and succeeded in accumulating some savings. He eventually returned to Nigeria, and was there when the railway was extended to northern Nigeria. He remembered the part played by the railway in the spread of the cocoa industry in the Gold Coast, and he foresaw that railway development in Nigeria would revolutionize the prospects of the groundnut industry. He set up as a groundnut buyer and built up an organization of sub-buyers throughout the area. He provided these with cotton piece-goods, both as a means to purchase groundnuts and as inducement goods for their cultivation. He has contributed greatly to the spread of the industry. His activities and success are examples of the result of superior perception of economic opportunity.

The role of change in throwing into relief differences in economic performance may also apply internationally. The industrial revolution was the culmination of a long process of development. Nevertheless, the resulting changes, especially the technical advances, may have increased the relevance of differences in attitudes and aptitudes between peoples and individuals, and this may be an important factor in international differences in economic progress.

These differences in economic quality and performance are also relevant to overpopulation and population pressure. There is heavy emigration from the West Indies, which are said to be severely overpopulated. Yet the Lebanese are anxious to migrate to the West Indies, and those few who are admitted generally prosper and accumulate capital. Thus even at current levels of technique the West Indies are not overpopulated in terms of Lebanese although they are in terms of West Indians. There are many similar examples in the underdeveloped world.

The rapid growth in range and effectiveness of restrictive tendencies in underdeveloped countries is an important feature of the economic landscape which, in the same way as personal and racial differences in economic performance, are rarely mentioned in polite economic society. They are also among those important facets and factors of economic life which do not lend themselves readily to quantification, which may partly account for the inclination to ignore them. Although xenophobia and tribal, racial, and national sentiments may partly underlie these measures and tendencies, they are largely examples and expressions of the economic restrictionism of specialized societies, which may emerge even when specialization, though it has made some headway, is still incomplete. In societies in which there is some specialization people frequently try to increase the scarcity value of their services by restricting entry of others into their own or related activities, because by such restrictions each specialist group can improve its relative position and, up to a point, also its real income. Moreover, the beneficiaries of such measures tend to overestimate the advantages they derive from them, while those who are disadvantaged generally do not fully perceive their disadvantage: people are far more aware of the competitive aspect of the relationship between themselves and other people than they are of the relationship of complementarity. This leads many people to accept or even to support restrictive measures which do not benefit them or may even harm them.

Restrictive measures have become much more significant and effective with the extension of government intervention in economic life, because government support is frequently a condition of their effectiveness and their maintenance. Public opinion, particularly influential opinion, generally readily supports restrictionism, and indeed its acceptance may give governments far less trouble than attempts to resist the pressure. Administrators may welcome restrictive measures for these reasons, as well as for others, such as the closer official control it makes possible over economic life and the apparently tidier system which results from them.

Although for political and administrative reasons such measures are most effective and popular when directed against foreigners and members of racially or linguistically distinct groups, they are quite often directed against members of the local population also. The foreigners or minority groups whose activities these measures are designed to restrict are usually people of little actual or potential political power, so that these measures are not motivated by fear of possible political domination by these groups. Of course when such measures are directed against members of the local population the question of foreign political influence does not arise at all.

Restrictive measures affect adversely both the allocation of resources and the growth of resources and of income. They also aggravate the unemployment stemming from the lack of co-operant resources, because they prevent the most effective deployment of available capital and skill and they also retard the growth of these resources. By narrowing markets they increase the frequency and severity of local shortages, especially of food, and retard specialization, production for the market, and thus the growth of the economy.

These measures which are now so effective have been introduced in underdeveloped countries at a comparatively early stage. Indeed, many underdeveloped countries, especially in Africa, have hardly emerged from the restrictionism characteristic of tribal xenophobia before being overtaken by the restrictionism characterized by more definitely economic motives. Thus these economies have not experienced the comparatively long spell of relatively unrestricted economic activity undergone by developed countries in the past; this early emergence of effective economic restrictionism may appreciably retard their rate of economic progress.

Restrictive licensing of transport, which effects both local and foreign-owned enterprises, and which is in force in many British dependencies in Africa and Southeast Asia, is illuminating in this context. The measures are generally modeled on those introduced in the United Kingdom in the interwar period, which were designed mainly to maintain railway revenues and the wages and working conditions of road haulage workers. Their introduction in underdeveloped countries is anomalous in view of the obvious importance of cheap transport and of accessibilty in the promotion of development, and in view also of the large sums which are being spent in these countries on the improvement of roads and other communications.

Restrictive measures are generally sought by both labor and capital. In recent years one manifestation on the side of labor has become specially important. This is the introduction and maintenance of institutionally fixed minimum wages, whether by government or by trade unions, both as an instrument of restrictionism and as its partial objective. In certain special conditions the principal effect may be the transfer of otherwise assured monopsony profits from employers to wage earners, without any substantial effect on employment. But in the great majority of instances the volume of employment is almost certain to be affected, both through the retardation of the growth of the particular industry, and through the adoption of more capital-intensive methods of production.[14]

These institutionally fixed wage rates apply only to organized employment, and they are generally more effective in large establishments than in smaller enterprises, especially those owned locally. They do not apply to domestic service, small-scale agriculture, nor of course to self-employment; these are the ac-

14. The adoption of more capital-intensive methods of production is sometimes welcomed as providing impetus to technological change which is thought to raise the economy to a higher plane. As a corollary, the raising of money wages is commended as contributing to this desired result. This argument ignores, among other relevant factors, the depressing effects on wages of the overcrowding in the activities into which are forced the displaced workers, and the resulting retardation of mechanization there. Considerations of the allocation of existing resources may not suffice to provide criteria for policies designed to accelerate growth. But it does not follow that inflation of the money cost of labor in excess of its real cost (as measured by its opportunity cost) in some mysterious way conduces to growth to offset the wasteful allocation of resources to which it gives rise.

tivities, besides unemployment, into which are forced those who fail to secure employment in the restricted trades.

The effectiveness and results of institutionally fixed wages are important and little explored fields of economic study of underdeveloped countries. As I have said already, they are generally less effective, and often even altogether ineffective, in the smaller, locally owned establishments. But, of course, even when the wage rates are observed, the actual results of their imposition may differ greatly from the apparent results. For instance, unless entry can be restricted, the attractive wage rates may lead to an influx of additional workers and earnings will be reduced even if wage rates are maintained. Again, part of the difference between wage rates and the supply price of labor may be transferred from the workers to managers, foremen, and trade union officials in the form of bribes (kickbacks) to secure employment. In other instances the principal result may indeed be a transfer of monopsony profits from employers to workers. This, for instance, may be the result in those parts of Africa where there are only a small number of employers operating very large-scale enterprises and negotiating collectively, and where there is little in the way of alternative employment. But this is exceptional.

Cheap labor is an important asset of the underdeveloped countries, which by definition are poor in capital, skill, and developed natural resources. The inflation of the cost of labor beyond its supply price tends to retard development, especially the progress of industrialization. I know that it is most unpopular to say this, yet the operation of restrictive measures generally, and notably of this particular manifestation, is a very important and relevant aspect in which underdeveloped countries are at present hampered in economic development. Governments of underdeveloped countries often pride themselves on the establishment of minimum wages and maximum hours in certain branches of activity, but they say (and possibly understand) little of their effects on the rate of growth, the use of capital, or on the employment opportunities of those who have failed to secure employment.

There is a little-known but revealing episode of Commonwealth history which bears on this matter. Factory production of textiles began to make headway in India in the 1870's. There was an agitation in Great Britain for the introduction of statutory minimum wages and maximum hours in Indian industry, and for the establishment of higher standards in the Indian cotton and jute factories. Indian industrialists pointed out that these demands, apparently motivated by humanitarian instincts, largely reflected the desire of manufacturing interests in Lancashire and Dundee to raise the costs of their competitors. These protests helped to defeat the proposals, the acceptance and enforcement of which at that time would have substantially retarded Indian industrialization.

Most of the restrictive measures affect adversely the agricultural population, especially the producers of cash crops. The overcrowding in agriculture is aggravated by restrictions on employment opportunities outside it which result from institutionally fixed money wages, and also from restrictive licensing of transport, trading, and processing enterprises. These restrictions also raise the cost of the services used by producers of cash crops, and they retard the growth of the market for these products. The disproportionate burden of the cost of these measures on the agricultural population compared with the urban population is not accidental. The restrictions are examples of the result of the greater political influence and consciousness of their own interests of substantial sections of the urban population. This is an important feature of the social and economic landscape of underdeveloped countries which comes as a surprise to those who think in terms of European and American politics. In the underdeveloped countries the politicians treat the agriculturalist as a milch cow, while in developed countries he is treated as a pampered favorite. The difference in the distribution of political power is also often reflected in the incidence of taxation, which in underdeveloped countries tends to be much heavier on the rural population than on urban population with similar incomes (the taxation of foreigners being an exception). An important example is the very heavy taxation of the peasant producers of export crops in Asia and Africa, levied largely through the surpluses of official export monopolies, and the imposition of export taxes at very high rates. These influences are curiously reflected in the interpretation of the meaning of stabilization in measures affecting agriculture. In western countries this has come to mean the establishment of a floor, in underdeveloped countries the imposition of a ceiling. This has prompted the informal but informative remark by Professor Paish of London University that in overdeveloped countries you overpay farmers, and in underdeveloped countries you underpay them.

But by the last few remarks, I have already strayed into the field of policy, or at any rate very near to it; and such issues belong to the next lecture.

3

Some Issues of Policy

> A man has no more right to an opinion for
> which he cannot account than to a pint of
> beer for which he cannot pay. G. M. YOUNG

> For we must never abdicate before misdirected
> popular enthusiasm.   PIETER GEYL

THE PROPOSITIONS of positive economics do not lose
their relevance when we consider economic policy,
that is, the field of normative economics and the art
of political economy. They are, indeed, indispensable
both for the rational framing of particular measures
and for the assessment of the implications of wider
issues of policy. But although these propositions are
indispensable, they are also on several grounds insufficient. When correctly interpreted, the conclusions
of positive economics are independent of political
positions; but they are also insufficient for policy
recommendations. The merits and wisdom both of
specific measures and of more general courses of
policy depend on their effects on the total social situation, and not only on those aspects with which econo-

mists are primarily concerned. And, more fundamentally, assessment of policies is deeply influenced
by political positions and by value judgments, most
notably by one's view of the kind of society one prefers. But these considerations do not affect the assessment of all measures and policies equally. For
instance, they do not affect significantly the assessment of many specific measures of policy, such as those
which I shall examine shortly. But they do affect
greatly the assessment of pervasive policies such as extensive compulsory saving, which I shall consider subsequently.

I intend first to discuss certain measures
and courses of action which can be assessed fairly conclusively with the minimum intrusion of political
preferences and judgments, and then to proceed to
broader issues in the assessment of which political
positions and value judgments are increasingly relevant as they become wider and broader. When such
issues are considered, the topics could indeed be
labeled more appropriately dilemmas of policy, rather
than issues of policy. This is because even if the
results of the different courses of policy were clearly
predictable, the choice of one or another cannot
usually be unambiguously stated to be the right choice,
since people do not agree on the importance to be
attached to different component elements of the result; in addition, the outcome usually cannot be
clearly predicted. The striking of a balance between
conflicting advantages, disadvantages, and risks of
different courses of action involves value judgments,

considerations of economic analysis, assessment of political and administrative possibilities in the special local circumstances.

The difficulties of judgment or prediction are the greater because these considerations have to be applied to the possible results of the different policies on the total social situation, and not only to those which fall within the special purview of the economist. As far as possible I shall try to indicate the relative importance of these considerations in the assessment of the issues examined. The policies and measures to be discussed are widely canvassed or applied in underdeveloped countries, and they are also issues on some or all aspects of which the economist is qualified to express an opinion.

In many underdeveloped countries of the Commonwealth measures are in force, largely introduced during the last fifteen years, which prohibit the export, or even the local sale, of produce falling below certain physical standards. An analogous measure is the practice of the export monopolies in Africa of prescribing price differentials which are unrelated to market criteria and prices, paying large premiums for certain grades of output and subjecting others to heavy discounts purely on the basis of certain physical standards. These measures are intended to encourage the production of output reaching certain physical standards and to discourage or even prevent the production of lower grades. In some instances even the establishment of local processing plants has been barred on the ground that they would use low grade produce which is deemed undesirable, even though these products have a value in world trade. These policies reflect the familiar failure to distinguish between technical and economic efficiency by placing the emphasis on physical standards irrespective of the value of resources required for their attainment.[1] As the physical standards are divorced from market considerations these practices are wasteful: they induce uneconomic expenditure of effort, discourage production which would be economic, and retard production for sale. Any improvement of quality thus effected differs fundamentally from improvement in quality resulting from improved technical knowledge. There are by now important political, administrative, and commercial interests involved in the maintenance and operation of this system.

The payment of uniform prices to producers irrespective of their location, and the charging of uniform freights irrespective of distance, are practices which have been widely adopted in British African territories. They encourage production distant from the ports and consuming centers, and discourage nearby production. This means that a given volume of output absorbs an unnecessary volume of transport resources. This results in uneconomic use of resources, because some of the production which takes place would not have been undertaken if the producers had

1. These are not monopolistic measures to restrict supply and raise the price under the guise of raising standards. The proportion of total market supplies affected is much too small for this purpose.

had to bear the full cost of production and transport, so that the value of this output is less than that of the scarce resources used in its production.[2]

In the British territories in Southeast Asia a system of land charges is in force which in its operation and results is somewhat similar to the charging of freights irrespective of distance. For instance, in Malaya unused land is owned by the government; when it is alienated for cultivation the authorities charge a capital sum and an annual payment (the latter known as quit rent), neither of which varies with location or fertility, but only with the kind of crop which is to be cultivated. Because these payments do not vary with location and fertility they often exceed the net yield of which the land is capable, so that the land remains uncultivated even though it could contribute to output. The annual payments are clearly not rents in the accepted economic sense, and the misnomer may have obscured the implications of the system, including its wasteful results.

I should like to refer briefly to another measure of policy in force in Malaya. With exceptions which are both irrelevant and insignificant, no land has been alienated there for rubber planting for well over a quarter of a century; this in a country four-fifths of which is still jungle, and which (because it produces

2. Nor does this system simplify administration; quite the reverse. Its administration is generally also wasteful because the actual transportation is often undertaken by intermediaries or transport agencies who have to be reimbursed by the authorities for the cost actually incurred, which requires elaborate filing and checking of claims which would not be necessary in the absence of this system.

less than one-third of the world's output of natural rubber and has no control over planting elsewhere) cannot hope for monopoly gains from restricting capacity. This policy of refusing to allow more land to be used for rubber planting is anomalous. It affects adversely the future supply of Malayan rubber and raises its cost of production. It bars a very important category of investment in agriculture in the production of a crop especially suitable for cultivation by the Asian smallholder. Quite apart from the very large numbers of landless laborers in Malaya, there are also tens of thousands, possibly hundreds of thousands, of cultivators who have no rubber smallholdings or other properties producing comparably profitable cash crops. Even when a man has a rubber smallholding, his children, with the exception of one son, will generally still have to go without, a consideration of some importance in view of the rapid population growth in Malaya.[3] Not surprisingly, the land offices receive many applications for the alienation of land for rubber cultivation, and the number of applications would be much larger still if it were not widely known that they are usually refused. Whatever part the political power of European estates may have played in the past in the introduction of this policy, this has nothing to do with the situation today. The principal reason for its continued maintenance is almost certainly the official reluctance to face the

3. Both the economic effects and the wider social and political implications of this policy are examined at some length in my article "Malayan Rubber Policy," *Political Science Quarterly*, LXXII (March 1957), 83-99.

disastrous implications of a policy which has been pursued so long; it presents an instructive example of the self-perpetuation of a policy when the circumstances in which it originated have long passed.[4]

This anomalous policy in turn recalls the wider problem of conservation, which is another fertile field of confusion of physical and economic criteria which serves to retard development in many countries of the Commonwealth. The widespread idea that there is something inherently desirable in keeping assets in a particular physical form is an extreme case of the more general idea that the rate of utilization of these assets should be governed by physical criteria instead of economic criteria designed to maximize the net returns over their life. Yet this idea widely influences conservation policy, both in the rate of utilization of publicly owned resources, and through official measures prescribing the rate of utilization of privately owned resources designed to encourage their maintenance in a particular physical form or to extend their life (for instance by special taxation designed for these purposes).[5] It is worth remembering that those in charge of conservation measures may have vested interests in the extension of the life of the asset, and in the insistence that its rate of utilization should be governed by physical criteria.[6]

4. I believe that both the ban on the alienation of land for rubber planting and the system of uniform quit rents are in force also in British Borneo.

5. More extensive discussion of these particular issues of conservation policy will be found in Yale Brozen, *Textbook for Economics* (Dubuque, Iowa, 1948), chap. xxxii.

6. Conservation is sometimes urged as an argument in support

Measures such as the prescription of standards of quality divorced from consumer requirements and market considerations, or the introduction of uniform price systems and the charging of freights irrespective of distance, or of rents irrespective of location or fertility, or the framing of conservation policies based on physical criteria reflect primarily a failure to appreciate the relevance and effects of costs and prices, and perhaps even a failure to appreciate that money payments generally reflect the acquisition or use of scarce resources. I do not want to be misunderstood here. I am not suggesting that policy should be guided by a simple acceptance of market prices, or that these imply an ideal allocation of resources. The present point is a wholly different one: it is that policy cannot be framed rationally unless the effects and implications of prices, including price changes and differentials, are considered.

This applies far beyond the measures I have already instanced. It is clearly relevant to taxation in general, as has been widely recognized in the field of taxes on consumption, in which in the past at any rate the response of demand has usually been considered a material factor in discussions of public finance in developed countries.

---

of the refusal to alienate land for rubber planting in Malaya. This is hardly to be taken seriously, since not only is four-fifths of the country uncultivated, but, additionally, the cultivation of a tree crop takes practically nothing out of the soil. Especially (but not only) on smallholdings, it is largely the replacement of one type of forest by another and this does not raise the issues usually associated with the utilization of a wasting asset.

In recent academic and official literature on the economic problems of underdeveloped countries the repercussions of prices and price changes on both supply and demand have come to be widely ignored; proposals for such measures as the imposition of import and export duties at high rates over a wide range of commodities have been advanced on the assumption that this does not affect either demand or supply. These effects have been ignored even in conditions in which substantial costs of transport and production ensure that both current production and the establishment of capacity are necessarily much affected by the price received by the producer; and also in conditions in which the limited nature of incomes ensures that the demand is necessarily affected by the price of the taxed products.[7]

In fact, these effects need to be considered with special care in underdeveloped countries, because development is generally much affected by the extension of the exchange economy. This in turn is necessarily influenced by the prices received by the producers and, more generally, by the relative attractiveness of the exchange and subsistence sectors. Taxation (other than in kind) is necessarily levied on the exchange sector, and, if the repercussions of prices and price changes are ignored, its effects cannot be assessed either on the extension of the exchange economy or on the supply of effort or saving. Its structure will not then be designed to obviate or minimize any adverse

7. Examples will be found in the references in chap. i, n. 6, above.

effects in this sphere which may stem from the raising even of necessary and desirable revenue, that is, revenue which may make possible desirable and productive expenditures.

Let me consider a few examples. Taxes on consumption will affect the extension of the exchange economy less if incentive goods are taxed relatively lightly. This factor is usually neglected in proposals for taxing inessentials, which are frequently precisely the incentive goods the attractiveness of which induces production for the market. Export duties and similiar levies will affect supply least if they fall on commodities of which the long-period supply is comparatively inelastic, for such reasons as the absence or low level of cash costs, or the absence of suitable alternatives open to the producers.[8]

These are not merely formal considerations: we often know enough about the conditions of supply and demand of different commodities to apply them in practice. For instance, export crops which are wild products as distinct from cultivated crops, such as West African palm-oil and palm-kernels, can be taxed without affecting the establishment of capacity. Again, the bulk of the supply of some crops may be produced in areas already largely absorbed by the exchange economy, or in areas near to the principal markets, or be produced by farmers without

8. This is because in these conditions the substitution effect of taxation is comparatively unimportant. But taxation of the exchange sector has to be carefully framed to ensure this result. Most of the export and income taxes in underdeveloped countries are more likely to bring about the opposite result; cf. n. 16 below.

easy access to comparable alternatives. In such circumstances export taxes are less likely to affect the extension of capacity and the spread of the exchange economy than does taxation of other cultivated export crops at comparable rates. The response of supply, though material, is of course not the only relevant consideration in the selection of the commodities to be taxed. The choice would be affected by various other factors and considerations, including those of equity. I stressed the response of supply because it is important and yet often neglected in this area of discussion and in the framing of policy, and also because of the obvious relevance of economic analysis in this context.

The presence of certain irreversible functional relationships on the side both of production and consumption may also be turned to good use in the framing of taxation. Though very high prices may at times be required to stimulate the establishment of productive capacity for certain crops, once the capacity has been established it may continue to be operated at appreciably lower prices; the establishment of plantations (both estates and smallholdings) of cultivated crops in remoter areas and their subsequent operation are a convenient example. Again, commodities for which the income elasticity of demand may be high may soon develop into conventional necessities for which the price and income elasticities of demand are much lower. Such considerations are material to the framing of a rational structure of taxation, though of course they are again not the only relevant considerations.

I now turn to the operation of the marketing boards in British Africa, which have a statutory monopoly over the principal export crops produced by the African population in these territories. When these boards were established, formal official undertakings were given that they would be used only to stabilize the prices received by producers over a period, and that they would on no account be used as instruments of taxation. However, from their inception these organizations developed into a system of severe taxation of the producers whom they were supposed to benefit. Various factors have contributed to this development. They included the discrepancy in political effectiveness and power of the urban and the rural population, the cleavage of interest between administrators and producers, and a desire to socialize saving. But the intellectual failure to ask certain relevant questions about the significance of prices and price changes has also been partly responsible. When these export monopolies were established, or rather put on a permanent basis, it was formally stated that they would withhold part of the sales proceeds from producers when prices were high, in order to pay them out when prices were low. However, no one seems to have specified or even asked what was meant by high and low prices, terms which are meaningless unless they are related to a base or norm. There are a number of other questions which were ignored, all essentially relevant to a discussion of stabilization and connected with the role of prices. These include the problem of distinguishing a fluctuation in prices from a change in the trend of prices, and, more generally, the problem of maintaining contact with the trend of prices, which reflect changes in the terms of trade, or in the value of money, or in the conditions of supply and demand of particular products. Nor were the effects considered on the establishment of capacity and on the progress of the exchange economy of withholding from producers a large proportion of sales proceeds. And this is a very incomplete list of the relevant questions which were ignored.

The same neglect of the role of prices which has been partly responsible for the development of the system into a machinery of taxation prevents it from making the most effective contribution to the development of these economies. This is because it leads to a disregard of the effects of the system on the long-term supply of the taxed products and, more generally, of its effects on the extension of the exchange economy. Unless stabilization is clearly defined such an outcome is quite probable, since without clear definition stabilization is a meaningless, omnibus expression, capable of a number of different, and indeed conflicting, interpretations.

The development of agricultural price stabilization into a system of taxation is no novelty. I cannot resist quoting some passages brought to my notice by Dr. H. Myint, of Oxford University, describing such a development in China in the eighth century of the Christian era. The passages embody some observations by Po Chü-i, scholar and administrator of that period:

In 736 a system called Harmonising (or as we should say 'stabilising') Purchase was introduced. The Government bought grain at above the market rate in years of good harvest, when the peasants were suffering owing to the low price of grain, and sold it below the market rate in bad years. Po, who at that time had no administrative experience, shows himself thoroughly in favour of such a measure. Years afterwards he realised, as we shall see, that if sale to the Government was obligatory and if the Government paid in media of ambiguous value (such as rolls of stuff which, although of the specified length, might be in such bad condition as to be worthless) Harmonising Purchase easily degenerated into being a camouflaged form of unauthorised taxation.

. . . Among the various devices for raising revenue was the so-called Grain Harmonisation. There had been a system in the 8th century by which, in order to steady the price of grain, the Government bought up grain in good years at more than the current price and put it on the market in bad years at less than the current price. Gradually this developed into a system of forced sale to the Government at an arbitrary price, paid in media that were of little value to the recipient—for example, lengths of silk and cloth not of standard quality, which were difficult to dispose of. In a Memorial to the Throne dating from about 808, Po claims to have knowledge of this system from two angles: 'I once lived for some time in a small country place where I was registered as a contributor to this scheme and was myself treated with great harshness. More recently, on the other hand, one of my duties when employed at a small place near the Capital was to direct the operations of those who were "harmonising," and I found that if there was any recalcitrance, the whip was used. . . ."[9]

However, it would be quite wrong to instance this episode, together with its present-day counterpart, as confirming the Biblical remark that there is nothing new under the sun. There is no evidence that the administrators and the intelligentsia of the period maintained that this system benefited the cultivators.

In underdeveloped countries the absence of a highly developed administrative apparatus and the difficulties of effective consumer rationing at times pose problems which cannot be handled effectively unless the response of consumers and intermediaries to prices and price differences is recognized. I mentioned in my first lecture the operation of price control over bicycles in the Gold Coast in the early years after the Second World War. I described the emergence of windfall profits in the distributive chain between the stages of partially effective price control and the final retail sale, which was generally at the open market or equilibrium price, and I also mentioned the resulting rush for supplies. Such a situation, which is characteristic of the operation of price control in underdeveloped countries, often results in great administrative and political strain, and at times even in acute tension, particularly when the larger

9. Arthur Waley, *The Life and Times of Po Chü-i, 772-846 A.D.* (London, 1949), pp. 22 and 60-61.

merchants are foreigners. The windfall profits and the excess demand can be removed if indirect taxes are imposed, or raised sufficiently to bridge the gap between the supply price of the available merchandise and the equilibrium price at which the available supply and the quantity demanded balance. This resolves the difficulties stemming from the excess of demand over available supply at the ruling price, and it does this without raising the price to the great majority of the consumers who in any case pay the open market price.[10]

I have discussed the measures of policy reviewed so far essentially in economic terms, largely without reference to wider political considerations. I believe that this approach was legitimate in an examination of these particular policies and of their results.[11] It would be less appropriate to an assessment of the restrictive measures which I discussed towards the end of the last lecture. Especially where these are designed to restrict the entry, activities, and operations of foreign personnel or capital, they clearly have to be assessed partly or largely on considerations which are outside economics. But even in these conditions their effects and incidence cannot be appreciated with-

10. Indeed the price paid by most consumers might be reduced because of the deflationary effect of the imposition of additional taxation.

11. The development of stabilization policy into a system of taxation has far-reaching political implications besides the technical economic considerations already discussed. These wider results and implications, some of which are mentioned briefly later in this chapter, reinforce the conclusion derived from more specifically economic analysis.

out economic analysis. Restrictive measures rarely reflect a systematic policy designed to benefit the local population against foreigners; indeed, foreigners are often important beneficiaries, since they may own and operate many of the enterprises shielded from competition. In short, these are measures in the assessment of which economic considerations, though not exclusively sufficient, are clearly material.

I now turn to somewhat wider issues, to the production of cash crops as an instrument of economic development and the scope of government action in this sphere. The relative merits of the production of cash crops and of industrialization as instruments of economic development cut across the issue of government control over economic life. In the economic history of many western countries there have been instances of rapid industrialization with very little government intervention; conversely, there have been many examples of close control over the activities of the producers of cash crops, from the days of ancient Egypt to the contemporary Gezira scheme in the Sudan, under which the tenant farmers producing cotton are very closely controlled by a statutory corporation.

In my last lecture I referred briefly to the wide range of policies in underdeveloped countries of the Commonwealth and elsewhere which adversely affect agricultural producers, especially producers of cash crops. Although these policies are not all directly designed to restrict the development of cash crops, in the course of the last few years a variety of influential criticisms have been explicitly raised against reliance on this type of production as an instrument of development. I shall consider some of these, because they tend to serve as specious intellectual bases or rationalizations for policies which in the event do affect adversely the producers of cash crops.

The various criticisms are really variants of a single theme, namely that the low incomes of those underdeveloped countries which are large producers or exporters of cash crops show that this activity does not serve to promote development. I have already referred in my previous lecture to some of these variants: the suggestion that the low level of income is evidence of stagnation; or that the advanced sectors of these economies are merely enclaves with capital and skills supplied from abroad; and that agricultural production has not promoted the growth of capital. I need not go over this ground again. I might repeat, however, that most of this confuses a late start on the road to progress with stagnation; that it neglects the fact that large portions of the economy are outside the exchange sector; and that it overlooks important categories of capital formation.

There are one or two other variants of the general theme. One deprecates substantial production of cash crops for export on the grounds that primary producers somehow face inherently deteriorating terms of trade; and this is sometimes supported by reference to an alleged deterioration in the terms of trade of primary producers from the 1870's to the 1930's. It is hard to make sense of this opinion, and I want to mention only the most obvious objections. The statistics quoted are almost wholly emptied of significance by the fact of fundamental changes in the conditions of production, such as the shift in rubber production from that of a South American wild crop to that of an eastern plantation crop (to mention only one instance), so that the figures are quite unrelated to factorial terms of trade. Even if these latter also had deteriorated, it would not follow that this would continue in the future (in fact, of course, the movement has been quite different during the last twenty years); but even if it did, it still would not follow that other types of activity would yield more favorable results.

The other variant I want to consider is the suggestion that this form of development is somehow stultifying, in that it peters out without setting up a cumulative process of growth, and notably that it fails to prepare the way for industrialization. This seems to be roughly the reverse of the truth. Nobody can foretell whether a particular process will be cumulative, and if so over what period; this is clear from the decline of countries which at one stage were very prosperous. Quite obviously, however, reliance on cash crops does not stand in the way either of cumulative growth or of industrialization. To mention but one contemporary example, in Malaya there is now appreciable industrialization made possible by the growth of skills and capital, and by the development of a market for simple consumer goods and agricultural implements based on the incomes generated by the production of cash crops. This is analogous to the growth of industry elsewhere, especially in Great Britain and North America, where industrialization followed the extension and improvement of agricultural production.

Production of cash crops represents generally less of a break with traditional methods of production than does industrialization at any early stage. Once the cultivation of cash crops has proceeded for some time, people get used to the ways of a money economy, which in turn promotes and facilitates industrialization. Thus agricultural production for the market in the early stages of development usually assists industrialization in various ways: by generating incomes and thereby providing a market for manufactures; by contributing to government revenues; by promoting the accumulation of private and public capital; and by promoting the development of the habits, skills and attitudes appropriate to a money economy. For these reasons industrialization emerging from production of cash crops is likely to be less costly, both in terms of economic resources and in terms of social strain, than if it proceeds without this preparation. Thus in this sense the production of cash crops and the development of industrialization are complementary.

There is another idea, or set of ideas, which is to some extent related to the criticisms of reliance on cash crops which I have already discussed. This criticism finds fault with production of cash crops, especially for export, on the ground that it exposes both the producers and the economy as a whole to un-warranted hazards. This suggestion also deserves a little examination, both because it raises interesting issues and because it is often influential. Contrary to some idyllic notions, a subsistence economy is not one which is secure and snug, and which provides its members with a modest but assured living. In any meaningful sense its hazards are much greater than those of an exchange economy. It normally operates on a very low level and has no reserves against ad-versity, either in the form of accumulated stocks or in the form of a high income which, even when reduced, still offers a tolerable standard of living, one which may indeed be comfortable. Moreover, such an economy has no access to external resources. It is not accidental that famine, pestilence, and similar disasters occur in subsistence economies and not in exchange economies. But although the haz-ards of a subsistence economy are far greater, they are generally much more readily accepted by the population because they are direct, obvious, appar-ently inevitable, and certainly not the responsibility of man. The monsoon fails and people starve. Con-trast this with a fall in export prices, or with a rise in the cost of living. The hardship is far less, but its causes are remote and are only too readily ascribed to incompetence and malice. The resulting political tension is particularly pronounced when the impact of a money economy has been rather sudden, so that while the people respond to it very readily they find its rationale difficult to understand. The more critical attitude towards the hazards of an exchange economy is also an example of the more general issue that political contentment is not a simple function of the level of real income.

These political difficulties underline the importance of enlightening the population on the functioning of an exchange economy, and also of removing as far as possible the sense of dependence of the population on particular firms or groups of firms. When there is a high degree of concentration in trade, the merchant firms necessarily influence prices, even if in the absence of barriers to entry they cannot secure high profits; and where there are effective barriers to entry, the power to influence prices is, of course, much greater. In such circumstances the population is apt to feel a sense of dependence on the merchants and to ascribe adverse price changes (and all price changes affect adversely some people) to their malice. Such accusations are particularly likely to emerge and gain credence when these firms are foreign owned. In the absence of a high degree of concentration this particular strain is less likely to arise, which suggests that in these conditions measures likely to increase concentration in trade, or otherwise to endow traders with some monopoly power (as, for instance, restrictive licensing or the granting of zonal monopolies), need to be scrutinized with special care.[12]

12. The presence and nature of the risks of reliance on a few exports crops, and the possibilities and merits of price stabilization, accumulation of reserves and diversification of the economy are examined in Bauer and Yamey, *op. cit.*, chaps. xiv and xv.

I have repeatedly protested against the notion that underdeveloped countries are generally stagnant. But a recognition of this progress does not imply advocacy of *laissez faire*. Many acute problems arise from the impact of rapid and uneven change which may be held to justify government intervention. But they are quite different from those of stagnation. Rejection of the suggestion that underdeveloped countries stagnate or are caught in a vicious circle of poverty, and recognition of the presence of certain other problems, are matters which cut across the issue of government intervention in economic life in much the same way as does the question of reliance on cash crops or on industrialization as instruments of development.

First there is the task of influencing the institutional framework of economic activity. The emergence and spread of agricultural production for sale both require and bring about important institutional changes. Without suitable institutions the economy cannot function effectively; the shaping of these to accord with desired ends of policy devolves largely on the government, since this is a task which cannot be performed by individuals operating through the market. In the early stages of economic development when the economy has not yet been pervaded by the exchange economy, the problem of devising and shaping suitable institutions is likely to be especially important, complex and delicate. This is a vast and important subject. But in spite of its great importance and interest I cannot pursue it here. The results of particular institutional changes depend in a large measure on local conditions. Their advocacy depends on value judgments and on their probable effects on the total situation in the particular circumstances. Thus, the effects of changes which an Indian government may wish to introduce in the field of land tenure, and, even more important, in animal husbandry, might be most far-reaching. But advocacy of these depends fundamentally on value judgments, as well as on an assessment of their effects on the total social situation; it does not lend itself easily to economic discussion, least of all to economic discussion in general terms. But I repeat that this is in no way intended to belittle its importance, or the importance of careful inquiry and systematic reasoning in the framing of such measures.

The task of promoting a suitable and acceptable institutional structure is often exceedingly difficult. There is an illuminating discussion of some of these problems, especially in the field of land tenure, in the report of the Royal Commission on East Africa, which conveys the baffling dilemmas and difficulties in this area of policy. Difficult as are these problems in East Africa, they are likely to be even greater in India.

Even at the stage of economic development where cash crops play a prominent part there is much scope for useful, and indeed essential, government activity well beyond the shaping of institutions. I can mention only one or two of these possibly fruitful activities: their applicability to particular conditions depends very greatly on local circumstances, including the quality of the government and of its personnel. The activities I shall consider are not as important as some other more obvious tasks of government, such as the management of the currency, the provision of basic services which yield indiscriminate benefits, and so forth. They also include the provision of elementary education, public health services and the establishment of basic communications. I do not discuss these because the importance of their effective performance is common ground. Unfortunately, this does not mean that they are generally effectively performed. It is a familiar spectacle today in many parts of the underdeveloped world that administrations find time and interest in trying to control quite minute sectors of economic life, while they cannot perform the primary tasks of government.

I mention first the provision of appropriate agricultural extension services. The readiness of the African or Asian peasant to respond to profitable opportunities does not mean that he can acquire technical knowledge without external assistance. The provision of agricultural extension services generally devolves on the government, because much of the benefit accrues to people who cannot be made to pay for it; and the cost of collection for the provision of this service would in any case be extremely high in underdeveloped countries. Although the importance of this activity is increasingly recognized, much of it is often marred by confusion between technical and economic efficiency; the insistence on certain physical standards as tests of quality is an example. Technical experts from economically advanced countries where labor is generally expensive are particularly apt to confuse technical and economic efficiency.[13]

My second example, or rather suggestion, stems from the recognition of discrepancies in the optimum scale of production in establishing capacity and in operating it. In many types of production, but especially in agriculture, there are often important economies of scale in establishing capacity, but no such economies (or there may even be appreciable diseconomies) in operating it. This discrepancy is pronounced in certain branches of tropical agriculture, especially in rubber production (the most important phases of which have not been mechanized even on American-owned estates), and to some extent also in sugar-cane production. It is likely to widen with the development of bulldozers and tracked vehicles, and with the increase in the cost of supervision and of hired labor. The former development is likely to bring about economies of scale in the establishment of capacity, while the latter is likely to underline the diseconomies of scale in operating it. There are generally few or no local individuals or firms with sufficient capital to establish capacity by large-scale methods, while institutional or political factors may prevent its establishment by foreign capital and its

13. There is an interesting discussion of the importance and problems of agricultural extension work in underdeveloped countries in W. Arthur Lewis, *The Theory of Economic Growth* (Homewood, Illinois, 1955), chap. iv.

operation by members of the local population. In the absence of these alternatives, the establishment of capacity by a government agency, which could sell or lease it to local agriculturalists, might prove desirable. The advantage might, however, be offset by political disadvantages, such as the use of the organization as an instrument of political control over the agricultural population.

One topic in the sphere of government activity in economies in which the production of cash crops for export by small farmers is prominent is both so important, and also sufficiently within the purview of the economist, that I do not want to leave it unmentioned. This is the problem usually discussed under the heading of stabilization. But I have written so much on this subject in easily accessible publications that I must do no more than state my position. I believe that the smoothing of wide and discontinuous fluctuations in the prices and incomes of producers might offer important political, social, and economic advantages. But such measures are fraught with grave difficulties and disadvantages, and they are worth experimenting with only if the objectives are clearly defined and specific, and if stringent safeguards are established to prevent the policy from developing into a crude and inefficient system of taxation.

The effective performance of these necessary or desirable government functions is likely to strain to the utmost the meager administrative resources of the governments of underdeveloped countries. Indeed, in the great majority of underdeveloped countries the political system is unsuitable and the administrative resources insufficient for the effective performance of even the necessary government functions. In these conditions extension of government activities beyond these tasks results in a neglect of some necessary and appropriate government functions. Failure to perform these effectively in turn obstructs efficient operation of the private sector of the economy; and the short-comings of the private sector in these conditions are often spuriously adduced as justification of government control of economic life.

These simple considerations are widely disregarded in the literature on underdeveloped countries, even by writers who stress the frailty of the administrative apparatus. An example is presented by the frequent suggestions that the lack of entrepreneurial talent in underdeveloped countries compared to more advanced economies requires extensive government participation in economic life. Yet, if the economy is short of entrepreneurial talent, why should a supply be available to the government?

In sum, the range of government functions envisaged by the foregoing discussion is extensive; and it sets exacting tasks to the governments of underdeveloped countries which they generally find difficult to fulfill.

I now turn to the wide issues of policy generally discussed under the heading of compulsory saving or taxation for development.[14] Over a large part even of this wide field economic analysis still retains its relevance; this applies especially to the assessment of different types of taxation. But the acceptance or rejection of compulsory saving as a major instrument of policy for development is much affected by one's political position, and this is also likely to influence one's assessment of the probable outcome of particular courses of action. I must, therefore, first state briefly my political position as far as it is relevant here.

I regard the extension of the range of choice, that is, an increase in the range of effective alternatives open to people, as the principal objective and criterion of economic development; and I judge a measure principally by its probable effects on the range of alternatives open to individuals. This implies that the process by which development is promoted affects the assessment, and indeed the meaning, of the result. The acceptance of this objective means that I attach significance, meaning, and value to individual acts of choice and valuation, including the individual time preference between the present and the future; and my position is much influenced by my dislike of policies or measures which are likely to increase man's

14. Compulsory saving or special taxation are more appropriate terms than taxation for development, since it begs the question to assume that the taxation will contribute to development. In a sense even compulsory saving is an inappropriate term, since it is quite speculative whether the process will benefit the "savers." Special taxation is a much more appropriate term. But having registered this caveat or protest, I shall fall in with current usage and refer to compulsory saving.

power over man, that is to increase the control of groups or individuals over their fellow men.

Now it is arguable, and is indeed often argued on various grounds, that in this context individual choices and valuations have no real significance, or at any rate no relevance or only very limited relevance. This is argued, for instance, on the ground that individual choices are essentially a function of the social environment, which itself will be changed as a result of the development brought about by compulsory saving; and further, that from the social point of view the future is as significant as the present; and that the inequality of wealth and income vitiates the relevance of individual choices as criterion of policy. On this line of reasoning a government, or any other group of sufficient influence, can set targets to serve as criteria of development, partly or wholly unrelated to the desires of some or most of the individuals in the society, on the grounds that individual preferences are essentially irrelevant, or that they will be modified and the individuals will adjust themselves readily to the changed circumstances brought about by compulsory saving and its results; or that in any case the increase in future output will be sufficient to justify the present sacrifices.

I reject such an approach; and I believe that it would be also rejected by many others who reflect on the meaning of development. But this rejection stems from a political position, and it cannot be derived from economic analysis. As I have already suggested, it stems in part from my opposition to the

increase in man's power over man which is implicit
in the restriction of access to independent alternatives
open to people as producers or consumers, which in
turn is an usual, though not invariable, corollary of
compulsion in this sphere.

In economic terms it is the growth in desired output which corresponds to an increase in the alternatives available to individuals. The increase in the
national income is the conventional and convenient
approximation of this concept. How close an approximation it is depends, among other relevant considerations, on changes in the volume of goods and services,
and of real costs, outside the conventional national
income estimates; and also on such changes as those
in the proportion of output produced by factors of
production which are or are not subject to direction;
or in the proportion of output bought out of taxes or
out of freely disposable income; and on other factors
affecting the correspondence between the volume of
goods and services and the range of alternatives open
to the population. I have instanced some of these
factors in my first lecture as limiting the meaningfulness in certain contexts of the conventional estimates
of the national income, especially as an index of development or of welfare in some sense or other.[15]

15. The performance of particular sectors of the economy, such
as the output of steel or of electricity or the volume of investment,
especially government investment, is frequently cited as an index
of economic development brought about by compulsory saving.
The use of this type of information for this purpose is open to all
the objections which can be raised to the use of national income
estimates, and to many other objections as well. Indeed, this
type of information is quite useless for a meaningful assessement
of the results of compulsory saving as an instrument of economic
development.

The advocacy of compulsory saving is generally along the following lines: economic development, which is axiomatically regarded as desirable, depends largely or wholly on the rate of capital formation; private capital formation is insufficient; desirable economic growth can be accelerated by increasing saving and investment through special taxation. Discussion of the merits of compulsory saving involves both economic and more general political considerations.   I shall begin with the former.   I shall consider, albeit briefly, both the collection and the expenditure of the funds.

Any contribution of compulsory saving to development must stem from a difference in the rate of development which results from control of these funds by the government, compared to that which would result from their retention in private hands. This is an involved and rather pompous way of putting the simple and obvious yet often neglected truism, that compulsory saving involves a transfer of resources; and that the process and its results can be assessed only if this is firmly and constantly remembered. Its merits are bound to be misjudged if the total proceeds of compulsory saving are seen as a net addition to resources, i.e., if they are considered to be costless. Yet this is the procedure in almost all development plans of underdeveloped countries, which usually regard government capital expenditure as a net addition to resources, and sometimes indeed even equate government capital expenditure with total investment in the country.

Taxation for development normally falls on activities in the exchange sector, and it is very likely to take forms which will retard the enlargment of production for wider exchange. This is the likely result of the taxation of incentive goods, or of the imposition of income taxes (particularly of graduated taxes), and especially of the imposition of export duties or similar levies on cash crops. Such measures bring into play the substitution effect between untaxed and taxed activities and enjoyments; subsistence production and leisure are untaxed, so that the levies are particularly likely to discourage effort, saving, and the transfer from subsistence production to production for wider exchange.[16] These results usually follow even where taxation results in reduced consumption, because in the early stages of the exchange economy the prospect of a higher or more varied level of consumption serves as a major inducement to invest. When, over wide areas, production is still largely for subsistence or for disposal in narrowly circumscribed local markets, export duties and similar levies affect directly the extension of the exchange economy because they reduce the area over which production for sale is possible. They also reduce both the wherewithal and the incentive to invest in the establishment, improvement, and equipment of agricultural properties, and in the purchase of simple tools and equipment.

16. The taxation of incentive goods, income taxes, and export duties all reduce the attractiveness of production for exchange compared to subsistence production. These measures also almost invariably affect marginal income proportionately more than total income, so that the substitution effect of taxation is likely to be pronounced.

Taxation for development contracts the supply of funds in the private sector, a result which, among other repercussions, reduces the capacity of individuals to finance, and thus to develop, local entrepreneurs.[17] The process usually also involves taxation which is both heavy and discontinuous, thus affecting the development of the sense of continuity which is a mainspring of the inclination to take the long view conducive to productive long-term investment.

In practice the likelihood that the taxation will have these adverse results is increased by the disregard of capital formation in agriculture, of the effects of prices on supply and demand, and of the problem and importance of extending production for the market. In particular, the neglect of important categories of capital and of the effects of prices necessarily prevents the assessment of the repercussions on private capital formation of both the collection and the expenditure of the funds. These instances of disregard prevent the framing of a structure of taxation designed to minimize the adverse repercussions.

Thus the proceeds of compulsory saving are not a net addition to the supply of capital. To regard them as such is to ignore the possible, and indeed likely, reduction in private capital formation which results both from the transfer of funds and from the disincentive effects of taxation. The overstatement of the

17. In principle the government may use the proceeds of taxation to finance private entrepreneurs. But this is unlikely to be of importance in the underdeveloped world at present or in the near future.

increase in the supply of capital is highly probable; and it is quite possible for compulsory saving to result in a reduction in total investment.

Moreover, it is misleading to think of investment as the only or the principal determinant of development. Other factors and influences, such as institutional and political forces, the qualities and attitudes of the population, and the supply of complementary resources, are often equally important or even more important. Heavy investment expenditure may result in little or no development; and conversely, substantial development may occur with the assistance of little investment. The importance of these other factors is necessarily understimated when investment is regarded as the key independent variable or factor in the promotion of development. And the neglect of these other factors may in turn result in policies which affect development adversely, such as the neglect of social and institutional factors and problems. It is more meaningful to say that capital is created in the process of development, rather than that development is a function of capital. This is clear not only from the obvious importance of institutional factors, of the economic qualities of the population, and of the availability of complementary resources, but it is also suggested by the composition of gross investment. Several of the components of investment are essentially items on which income is spent rather than propellants of the growth of income. Housing is an obvious and important example.

The expenditure of the proceeds of compulsory saving does not lend itself readily to general discussion. In certain circumstances it may be very productive, especially when the funds are spent for the provision of basic communications, education or agricultural extension work. But the presence of large surpluses over current expenditure is generally apt to lead to extravagance. And this is particularly likely to come about when development is seen largely as a function of investment, and when investment is measured solely by money expenditure regardless of its contribution to output. The pressures for conspicuous investment, for spectacular schemes, and for the adoption of methods emulating technically more advanced countries, are also likely to encourage economic waste. Thus both in the collection and in the expenditure of funds forces are at work to bring it about that the contribution of compulsory saving to development is not commensurate with the resources used.

These considerations still do not represent a conclusive case against compulsory saving. The taxation may be so designed that productivity or the supply of productive resources in the private sector are not affected adversely, or that any adverse effect is small. The public investment made possible may be very productive, and may be expected to result in an early and substantial increase in the national income.[18]   But

18. A special case of such productive investment would be provided by capital expenditure which enables the economy to

in such circumstances the government, if it believes in the advantages of the large-scale investment, can often (though not always) acquaint the population with the grounds for this belief; and the population will provide the saving voluntarily if it also attaches such a high value to the benefits to be expected. However, the advocates of compulsory saving would claim that the likely advantages of their proposals outweigh the sacrifices, and that they justify compulsory saving regardless of the possibility or practicability of eliciting the saving voluntarily. Altogether, the acceptance of this advocacy will depend on an assessment of the probable results of this course of action, both in terms of economic development and in terms of its effects on the total social situation; on the probable distribution of the benefits and costs of the process; and, most fundamentally, on value judgments about the meaning and significance of individual choices.

Thus, in the last resort assessment of the merits of compulsory saving depends unavoidably largely on political (value) judgments. Even if the funds are used most effectively and productively and the disincentive effects on the private sector are minimized, the process of development by this means implies direct compulsion which is absent when development takes place without it; that is, it implies direct compulsion, as distinct from social compulsions affecting

surmount a particular obstacle or hump in the path of development. Certain formal and practical considerations bearing on this case are examined at some length in Bauer and Yamey, *op. cit.*, chap. xiii.

individual choices. But as I have already said, there are many people who reject private choice and valuation as relevant criteria in assessing the merits of different processes of development; the acceptance or rejection of these criteria is essentially a value judgment, a judgment or preference stemming from a political position and not susceptible to technical economic analysis.

I now turn to wider social and political considerations which I think are relevant to the assessment of taxation for development, but which are not derived from technical economic arguments.

The right of some people to force others to develop is not self-evident, particularly when a widening of the range of choice, of access to alternatives, is regarded as the principal benefit of economic development, or at least one of its main advantages.[19] The practical relevance of this is underlined by the fact that those who insist on development are not those who bear its costs.

It is worth pausing on this for a moment. When people advocate accelerated development they are quite often unaware of the economic sacrifices and social strains implied. But even where these are appreciated, there is often a notable lack of correspondence between those who advocate taxation for de-

19. Professor Lewis is apparently among those who regard the widening of alternatives as the essential advantage stemming from economic development. "The advantage of economic growth is not that wealth increases happiness, but that it increases the range of human choice." Op. cit., p. 420.

velopment and those who pay for it. In underdeveloped countries the advocates are drawn very largely from among the urban population, while the sacrifices are imposed on the rural population. The lack of correspondence just mentioned is particularly pronounced and obvious when the advocates of accelerated development are foreign experts or visitors. Moreover, some of the most influential advocates of such measures often not only escape the sacrifices, but may even benefit from such policies in that they occupy the positions of influence and power, often accompanied by large incomes, which are created; they may get these benefits often entirely irrespective of economic performance.

We must therefore bear quite firmly in mind that those who so warmly advocate the imposition of sacrifices are not those who bear them. It is often said that heavy taxation for development is akin to a forced march, that is, the attainment of a desired goal by a painful process. This analogy is misleading on several grounds. One which is relevant is that in a forced march all march together; here some drive and others march.[20]

The insensitiveness of humanitarians to the results of their proposals is well known. The advocates of compulsory saving, who are so ready to disregard

20. It is often suggested that the sacrifices implicit in compulsory saving are similar to those which accompanied increased capital formation in the early history of the developed countries. This is misleading since in the history of these countries the process of capital formation was generally not accompanied by heavy taxation for this purpose nor by government prescription of the national output.

both the social strains and the economic sacrifices implicit in their proposals, exemplify the inhumanity of the humanitarians. Moreover, quite often the proponents of these heavy sacrifices have little or no roots in the community to which they wish to apply these drastic measures; often no roots in any other community either. The inhumanity of the humanitarians becomes more pronounced when it is reinforced by the ruthlessness of the rootless.

There is another political aspect of heavy compulsory saving which I want to consider, albeit only briefly. Such a policy generally results in a great inequality in the distribution of power within the country. Notably, it often greatly increases the power of particular groups of people over their countrymen, and it thus implies a restriction in the range of alternatives of those over whom the power is exercised. These implications of the system are quite general, but they are particularly obvious when the compulsory saving or special taxation is exercised by means of statutory export monopolies, the administrators of which closely control the incomes and the activities of producers. The weight we attach to this corollary of compulsory saving is obviously a value judgment, but it is relevant to an assessment of its merits.

This aspect of compulsory saving, the greater inequality in the distribution of power likely to result from it, is an example of a wider issue, which again should be obvious and yet is generally ignored.[21]

21. The possible, and indeed likely, increase in the inequality of power seems an important and little explored aspect of an

Even if compulsory saving does result in a substantial increase in the conventionally measured national income (compared to what this would have been otherwise), the political system and the nature of the society required for the process are likely to differ greatly from those which would accompany an increase in the national income without such drastic measures. This implication of the process tends to be overlooked in discussions which emphasize the national income as an index of well-being, and which suggest implicitly that the level of the national income somehow largely determines the character of the society. Of course it does nothing of the sort, as is obvious when a large part of economic activity is subject to direct government control. But the general consideration applies even more widely. The character of a society is governed by its historical development, by national and ethnic characteristics, by the political system, and by institutional arrange-

---

increase in the role of government in economic life. For various institutional reasons, such as the absence of a well-informed and effective public opinion and the differences in effectiveness between the urban and the rural population in many underdeveloped countries, this range of problems is of special importance in the underdeveloped world. But its relevance is wider. For instance, measures designed to promote greater equality in conventionally measured income and wealth may result in greater inequality of power among members of a society, notably in greatly increased power of some individuals or groups over others. This is obscured by the habit of regarding inequality of wealth as commensurate with inequality of power, notably as indicating the ability of some individuals to control others. In fact, freedom from control or dictation is a function of access to independent alternatives, and not of equality of wealth or incomes conventionally measured.

ments, to mention only some of the more obvious influences—that is, factors and influences other than the conventionally measured flow of goods and services. Societies in which the level of real income per head is about the same often differ widely in their modes of life. It is naïve to think that if incomes in the underdeveloped countries are increased by whatever means, their societies will reproduce those features and attributes of western countries which some people in these countries deem desirable. Emphasis on this important and often neglected set of considerations will not, I hope, be interpreted as a suggestion that the economic progress of the underdeveloped countries is not desirable, a suggestion which would indeed be quite contrary to the argument of these lectures.

I trust that I have not given the impression in this book that economics is of little use to the underdeveloped countries, or that preoccupation with underdeveloped countries cannot advance economic knowledge. On the contrary, I am convinced that it is a most fruitful and stimulating field for our studies. Although the landscape may at first be unfamiliar, the factors and influences from which our generalizations derive often stand out in clear relief; and work in this general area can powerfully extend and strengthen the generalizations of economics. This in turn will improve the prospects of successful assessment and prediction of the results of particular measures, which is the most effective contribution of the economist to the betterment of the conditions of people in the underdeveloped countries, as elsewhere.

I believe that we shall contribute most if we are not concerned too much with immediate issues of policy, that is, if we aim to promote knowledge rather than to promote policy. But even if they belong to the field of positive economics, our conclusions will often bear on policy; and it will help if we always set out their bases clearly. But whatever our chosen topic, we should go where the argument leads, irrespective of the popularity and political acceptability of our conclusions.[22] The readiness to do this has been a principal element in the phenomenal successes of the natural scientists. For various reasons, some of which I suggested in my first lecture, it is much more difficult to present the propositions of economics conclusively and convincingly. This adds to the temptation to fall in with what is readily acceptable to politi-

22. The political unacceptability or unpopularity of a conclusion does not mean that its proponent is less influential than are those whose views are more readily accepted (sometimes known as realists). There is often a high correlation between the advice tendered by an economist and the measures of policy adopted without this indicating that the adviser exercises influence in any meaningful sense. He may only advise policymakers to do what they would wish to do in any case. Indeed, he may have been selected as adviser because it was anticipated that he would tender the kind of advice which makes it easier for the policymaker to pursue the policy which he is in any case set on. Thus the apparently highly influential adviser in fact neither contributes to knowledge nor does he influence the course of events. Some penetrating reflections on this subject will be found in an article by Professor Clarence Philbrook, " 'Realism' in Policy Espousal," *American Economic Review*, XLIII (Dec. 1953), 846-859.

cal and public opinion, and this is apparent in economic discussions on underdeveloped countries.

I shall close by reminding you of some injunctions of Alfred Marshall's which those of us who are engaged in the study of the underdeveloped economies will do well to remember.

While taking an attitude of reserve towards movements that are already popular, you will incline to be critical of prophecies that are fashionable.[23]

And he also realized the corollary of such an attitude:

Students of social science must fear popular approval; evil is with them, when all men speak well of them. . . . It is almost impossible for a student to be a true patriot and have the reputation of being one at the same time.[24]

23. *Memorials of Alfred Marshall*, p. 306.
24. Quoted from an unpublished manuscript in *Memorials of Alfred Marshall*, p. 89.

SUGGESTIONS FOR READING

I NOTED in the first lecture the value of unprocessed material in the economic study of underdeveloped countries. Such material does not lend itself readily to inclusion in a reading list. Moreover, even a reasonably comprehensive reading list for such a vast area of study as the economics of underdeveloped countries cannot be presented within the compass of an appendix to a small book. Those who wish to consult a more detailed list are referred to *The Economics of Underdeveloped Areas* by Arthur Hazlewood (London, 1954), which is an annotated reading list on this general subject.

The suggestions for reading presented below are essentially introductory. Some general books are suggested first, followed by publications which bear on the major specific topics discussed in Lectures 2 and 3. Many of the publications, notably *The Theory of Economic Growth* by Professor Lewis, and *The Economics of Under-developed Countries* by Mr. Yamey and myself, contain many references to the literature, often to primary sources, or to material which embodies the results of first-hand enquiry.

There is much material of interest to students of the

economics of underdeveloped countries in economic and anthropological periodicals, particularly *Economic Development and Cultural Change,* a journal published by the Research Center in Economic Development and Cultural Change, University of Chicago. The *Statistical and Economic Review* of the United Africa Company, though of more specialized interest, often carries much informative material.

Economists, especially those already familiar with some underdeveloped country, can benefit greatly from studies by competent anthropologists and also from accounts of perceptive travelers. Such literature often illuminates important and characteristic aspects of particular societies and regions. There are a number of references to such literature in the Cambridge Economic Handbook by Mr. Yamey and myself.

I. *General Reading*

P. T. Bauer and B. S. Yamey, *The Economics of Underdeveloped Countries,* London, 1957 (Cambridge Economic Handbook); S. Herbert Frankel, *The Economic Impact on Underdeveloped Societies,* Oxford, 1953; W. Arthur Lewis, *The Theory of Economic Growth,* London and Homewood, Ill., 1955; Vera Anstey, *The Economic Development of India,* 4th edition, London, 1952; W. K. Hancock, *Survey of British Commonwealth Affairs,* Vol. II, Part 2, London, 1941; *East Africa Royal Commission Report,* London, 1955.

The first three books in this list, though by economists and dealing primarily with economic aspects and problems of underdeveloped countries, treat these in a wider context, and generally consider factors and influences often relegated to institutional literature. The other three publications, though dealing specifically with particular areas, discuss a wide range of problems of general interest to the students of underdeveloped economies.

II. *Reading on Special Topics*

(i) *The Impact of Rapid Change*

The rapid economic changes in many underdeveloped countries over the last half-century and their implications are frequent themes of the literature of anthropology and sociology. These topics are also examined in every one of the books listed above under suggestions for general reading. They are also considered in Lord Hailey, *An African Survey*, London, 1938; and in my book *West African Trade*. There are many suggestive remarks on the social and political implications of rapid change in underdeveloped countries in Harry D. Gideonse, "Colonial Experience and the Social Context of Economic Development Programs," in Robert A. Solo (ed.), *Economics and the Public Interest*, New Brunswick, N. J., 1955, pp. 247-267; Eric Hoffer, *The True Believer*, London, 1951; B. F. Hoselitz (ed.), *The Progress of Underdeveloped Areas*, Chicago, 1952; E. Warner, *Trial by Sasswood*, London, 1955.

(ii) *The Measurement of National Income in Underdeveloped Countries*

There is a very good discussion of this subject in A. R. Prest and I. G. Stewart, *The National Income of Nigeria, 1950-51*, London, 1953. Other important discussions include: J. R. N. Stone, "Definitions and Measurement of the National Income and Related Totals" in *Measurement of National Income and the Construction of Social Accounts*, United Nations, Geneva, 1947; P. Deane, *Colonial Social Accounting*, Cambridge, England, 1953; International Association for Research in Income and

Wealth, *Income and Wealth*, Series III, Cambridge, England, 1953.

Some of the relevant conceptual problems in this context are discussed in Bauer and Yamey, *op. cit.*, Chapter II, and S. Herbert Frankel, *op. cit.*, Chapter III, and Simon Kuznets, *Economic Change*, London, 1954.

(iii) *Population*

Various aspects of population growth in underdeveloped countries are discussed in Bauer and Yamey, *op. cit.*, Chapter V, and Lewis, *op. cit.*, Chapter VI. The views of a number of well-known writers in this field are included in a collection of ten papers, *Modernization Programs in Relation to Human Resources and Population Problems*, Milbank Memorial Fund, New York, 1950.

There are widely differing interpretations by different writers of the implications of population growth in underdeveloped countries. Apart from the references just listed, the following may be cited: Colin Clark, "Population Growth and Living Standards," *International Labour Review*, LXVIII (1953), 99-117; D. G. Karve, *Poverty and Population in India*, London, 1936; K. Smith, "Some Observations on Modern Malthusianism," *Population Studies*, VI (1952), 92-105; J. J. Spengler, "The Population Obstacle to Economic Betterment," *American Economic Review*, XLI (1951), 343-354; J. J. Spengler, "Demographic Patterns," in H. F. Williamson and J. A. Buttrick (eds.), *Economic Development: Principles and Patterns*, New York, 1954, pp. 63-103.

(iv) *Capital and Economic Development*

The relation between capital formation and economic development is perhaps the most widely canvassed single topic in the general literature on economic development and underdeveloped countries. The subject is extensively discussed in the first three books listed under the suggesttions for general reading.

Important discussions of the general subject include: William Fellner, *Trends and Cycles in Economic Activity*, New York, 1956, Part V; Frankel, *op. cit.*, Chapters VII and VIII; L. M. Lachmann, *Capital and Its Structure*, London, 1956; Nurkse, *op. cit.*; Joan Robinson, *The Accumulation of Capital*, London, 1956; *Economic Progress*, Papers and Proceedings of a Round Table held by the International Economic Association (ed. by L. H. Dupriez), Louvain, 1955, with contributions by A. K. Cairncross, E. D. Domar, and Simon Kuznets.

(v) *Trading Activity in Underdeveloped Countries*

The role of traders in underdeveloped countries and the factors underlying the multiplicity of traders in many of these countries are topics which have recently emerged or re-emerged in the literature. They are discussed in Hancock, *op. cit.*, especially Chapter II; in my book, *West African Trade*; Bauer and Yamey, "Economic Progress and Occupational Distribution," *Economic Journal*, LXI (1951), 739-755; Sidney W. Mintz, "The Jamaican Internal Marketing Pattern," *Social and Economic Studies*, IV (1955), 95-103; S. Rottenberg, "A Note on Economic Progress and Occupational Distribution," *Review of Economics and Statistics*, XXXV (1953), 168-170.

(vi) *Restrictive Tendencies and the Effects of Institutional Wage Rigidities*

There are many references to these subjects in general economic literature but there is little systematic treatment.   Brief references or discussions of some wider relevance include: J. R. Hicks, *The Theory of Wages*, London, 1932, Chapter VI; W. H. Hutt, *The Theory of Collective Bargaining*, London, 1930; and *The Theory of Idle Resources*, London, 1939; D. H. Robertson, *Economic Fragments*, London, 1931; Barbara Wootton, *Plan or No Plan*, London, 1934, Chapter III; Henry Simons, "Some Reflections on Syndicalism," *Journal of Political Economy*, LII (1944), 1-25.

I have attempted a general discussion of restrictive tendencies in specialized societies in *West African Trade*, Chapter 3.

Restrictive measures, especially as they affect the employment of Africans, have been much discussed in publications dealing with various aspects of the economy of South Africa.   References include: Hancock, *op. cit.*, Chapter I; S. T. van der Horst, *Native Labour in South Africa*, London, 1942; and "Equal Pay for Equal Work," *South African Journal of Economics*, XXII (1954), 187-209.

The effects of institutionally fixed wages on occupational distribution and on economic development are discussed in several of the references just given, especially those dealing with conditions in South Africa.   They are also considered in the note by S. Rottenberg, already mentioned; and in my review of *Measures for the Economic Development of Under-developed Countries*, United Nations, New York, 1951, *Economic Journal*, LXIII (1953), 210-222.   These topics are also considered with special reference to the American South in various writings by Professor John V. Van Sickle, notably "The Wage Problem in the New South," *Georgia Review*, I (1947), 394-410; and "The South-East: A Case Study in De-

layed Industrialization," *American Economic Review,*
XLI (1951), 384-393.

(vii) *The Reform of Agricultural Marketing*

Various statutory measures (other than those designed
to stabilize or raise prices and incomes) are examined in
Bauer and Yamey, "The Economics of Marketing Reform," *Journal of Political Economy,* LXII (1954),
210-235.

(viii) *Economics without Prices*

Some implications for economics of conducting the discussion without reference to prices are examined in my
article, "The Economic Development of Nigeria," *Journal of Political Economy,* LXIII (1955), 398-411; and
"A Reply" [to Dr. John H. Adler] in the same journal,
LXIV (1956), 435-441.

(ix) *Government-Sponsored Industrialization*

There is an extensive literature on the controversial
subject of government-assisted industrialization in underdeveloped countries. There are many references to the
literature in the bibliography compiled by Mr. Hazlewood.
The subject is discussed at some length in Professor
Lewis's book, already mentioned, and in the Cambridge
Economic Handbook by Yamey and myself. Professor
Lewis has also dealt with the subject in "Industrial Development in Puerto Rico," *Caribbean Economic Review,* I (1949), 153-176, and "The Industrialisation of
the British West Indies," *Caribbean Economic Review,*
II (1950), 1-61.

Other publications include: H. G. Aubrey, "Small Industry in Economic Development," *Social Research,*
XVIII (1951), 269-312; H. Belshaw, "Observations

on Industrialisation for Higher Incomes," *Economic Journal*, LVII (1947), 379-387; N. S. Buchanan, "Deliberate Industrialisation for Higher Incomes," *Economic Journal*, LVI (1946), 533-553; J. Jewkes, "The Growth of World Industry," *Oxford Economic Papers*, III (1951), 1-15; P. N. Rosenstein-Rodan, "Problems of Industrialisation of Eastern and South-east Europe," *Economic Journal*, LIII (1943), 202-211; H. W. Singer, "Problems of Industrialisation of Underdeveloped Countries," in *Economic Progress* (ed. L. H. Dupriez), pp. 171-179.

(x) *Institutional Changes, Especially Changes in Land Tenure*

Various aspects of institutional change are discussed at length in all the books listed under general reading. There is an extensive discussion of the problems of land tenure in the *East Africa Royal Commission Report*. Perceptive discussion of certain aspects of institutional change include: L. P. Mair, "Modern Developments in African Land Tenure: An Aspect of Culture Change," *Africa*, XVIII (1948), 184-189; C. K. Meek, *Land Law and Custom in the Colonies*, London, 1946; Penderel Moon, *Strangers in India*, London, 1943.

(xi) *Price and Income Stabilization*

The smoothing of the impact of fluctuations in prices and incomes of primary producers, especially in underdeveloped countries, is discussed in two articles by Professor F. W. Paish and myself, "The Reduction of Fluctuations in the Incomes of Primary Producers," *Economic Journal*, LXII (1952), 750-780, and "The Reduction of Fluctuations in the Incomes of Primary Producers Further Considered," *Economic Journal*,

LXIV (1954), 704-729. The second article replies to criticisms of the first article, notably by Miss Peter Ady and Professor Milton Friedman, which appeared in the *Economic Journal*, LXIII (1953), 594-607 and LXIV (1954), 698-703.

The general issue of price and income stabilization is also considered by Sir Sydney Caine, "Instability of Primary Product Prices: A Protest and a Proposal," *Economic Journal*, LXIV (1954), 610-614; and in *A Reconsideration of the Economics of the International Wheat Agreement*, Food and Agriculture Organisation of the United Nations, Rome, 1952 (most of the economic analysis is by Mr. N. Kaldor). These publications also refer to a number of other contributions to the subject.

(xii) *Compulsory Saving*

This is discussed extensively in Professor Lewis's book and in the Cambridge Economic Handbook by Mr. Yamey and myself.

INDEX

Africa, relevance of economics to, 16; economic backwardness of, 20-21, 47, 49; increase of imports, 22; and bride prices, 24; economic progress in, 49-50, 51; exports from, 50-51, 58; and connection between trade and industry, 71-72; and restrictive measures, 79, 81; economic policies in, 87-88; marketing boards in, 96-97. *See also* Gold Coast; Kenya; Nigeria; Uganda

Agricultural extension services, 109-10

Agriculture, products of for sale and export, 58-59; and capital formation, 60-63; and restrictive measures, 83-84. *See also* Crops

Aristotle, 32

Art of political economy. *See* Political economy, art of

Asia, lack of economic achievement in, 48; economic progress in Southeast Asia, 49-50, 51; exports from, 51, 58; system of land charges in, 89. *See also* Ceylon; China; India; Malaya

Bacon, Francis, 46

Barriers to entry, 106

Bicycles, and price control, 16-17

Boom, and the law of demand, 10

Borneo, 91

Bride prices, 24

British Borneo. *See* Borneo

Capacity, establishment of, 93, 94, 95, 97, 110-11

Capital, control of in India, 17; scarcity of in underdeveloped countries, 68; creation of by migrants, 73-74. *See also* Capital formation; Investment

Capital formation, and agricultural production, 60-63; and the international demonstration effect, 64; and compulsory saving, 116-20. *See also* Investment

Nigeria, special premiums for products in, 8; bride prices in 24; and report of International Bank, 29; national income in, 50; exporting of products from, 50-51; trade in, 56; production of groundnuts in, 67-68, 75-76

Normative economics, 6-7, 33, 37, 42, 85

Nurkse, Professor Ragnar, 26, 64

Observation. *See* Direct observation

Oni of Ife, 56-57

Oracles, 30

Paish, Professor, 84

Palm-kernels, 51, 94

Palm-oil, 50, 94

Peanuts. *See* Groundnuts

Physical standards, 87-88

Po Chü-i, 98-99

Policies. *See* Compulsory saving, Conservation, Freights, Government, Industrialization, Land, Marketing boards, Physical standards, Prices, Rents, Restrictive measures, Taxation

Policy, and the economist, 6, 34-41 *passim*, 127; framing and assessment of, 85-87; and prices, 92

Political economy, art of, 6-7, 33, 37, 42, 85

Political position, as related to economics, 36-43 *passim*; and policy, 85, 86

Population, 53-54, 76

Port Harcourt, 56

Positive economics, defined, 6-7; and political position, 36-43 *passim*; and policy, 85-87; mentioned, 33, 42, 127

Poverty, 49, 64, 73

Power, unequal distribution of, 124-25

Prediction, as distinguished from forecasting, 10-11, 28; and the framing of policies, 87

Price control, 16-17, 96-100, 111

Prices, as related to demand, 8, 9, 10, 24, 29, 39-41, 93, 95; as related to supply, 8-9, 10, 24, 29, 39-41, 93, 95; control of, 16-17, 96-100, 111; changes of in underdeveloped countries, 20, 21; of brides, 24; as affected by custom, 24-25; government measures concerning, 87-89; and the framing of policy, 92; in an exchange economy, 93, 106; and the establishment of capacity, 95; attempts at stabilization of, 96-99, 111

Private sector, 120, 121

Production, increased by special premiums, 8; of cash crops, 59, 60-61, 63, 101-6, 117

Quantification, 12, 13, 14

Quit rent, 89

advanced countries, 26, 55-58, 64; low level of economic attainment of, 45-49; and national income, 49-50, 53-54, 126; growth of material progress in, 49-84 *passim;* trading activity in, 50-51, 56, 67-74, 102-3; agricultural production in, 58-59, 60-63, 83-84, 101-6; capital investment in, 60-63, 64, 68, 73-74; and international demonstration effect, 64-67; and the contributions of migrants, 72-76; restrictive measures used in, 76-84, 100-101; economic policies in, 87-126 *passim;* attempts at price stabilization in, 96-99; industrialization in, 103-4; and government economic functions, 111-12

Value judgments, 86, 87, 121
Values, 17, 18

Wages, 69, 80-81
Wants, pattern of in underdeveloped countries, 22-25, 26; increase of by international demonstration effect, 64

Xenophobia, 77, 79

Yoruban nation, 56